Kissinger

THE ADVENTURES OF SUPER-KRAUT

Kissinger ✠ ✠ ✠

THE ADVENTURES OF SUPER-KRAUT

Charles R. Ashman

LYLE STUART, INC., Secaucus, New Jersey

To my partner in this and all things
PAMELA

CONTENTS

PREFACE

In a way, this book was begun in 1956. At least, I began gathering the raw data then. Henry A. Kissinger had risen from Army private to Weapons Adviser to the Joint Chiefs of Staff. I was on Capitol Hill as a Congressional aide brought in by the Democratic majority. General Dwight David Eisenhower was President, and Richard Milhous Nixon was Vice President, but it was the legislative era of Bobby Baker and Lyndon Baines Johnson.

Everybody was swinging.

One night I was bearding for a Congressman. This is a duty of bachelor staff members when a legislator is married and wishes to go out publicly with a lady other than his wife. The Solon, the lady, and the bachelor staff member form a threesome. To the unsuspecting public, the bachelor (the "beard") is the lady's escort and the philandering lawmaker is just tagging along. Through this patriotic device, the domestic tranquility of the politician (as well as the Republic) is insured.

On this particular night, there were some variations on the theme. We were a foursome. The fourth member of our party was one of Washington's leading cocksmen, a Senator from Massachusetts. The Representative (my host) was pursuing the virtue of the wife of a Latin American Embassy official.

Ted Reardon, of the Kennedy Irish Mafia, brought over a pudgy professorial type to our group. The man's most memorable feature was on his arm—the tallest, most spectacular redhead I'd ever seen. She was a graduate student in Political Science, but looked like a Las Vegas show girl. He was Henry Kissinger, and looked like a Henry Kissinger.

The evening was rewarding. I got the South American. The Congressman got the graduate student. And the Senator got Kissinger. This is not to suggest that the late former Senator's fancies included men, but to point out that he was one of the few who would give up a party for a skull session.

Five years later the Senator became President. AMTRAK has no Metroliner that could have handled the Harvard-Washington shuttle crowd. President Kennedy's New Frontier needed high-level brainpower to balance his energetic political team. Kissinger was a natural. As a Jew, he appealed to the Kennedy concern for minorities in government. As a world-power scholar, he had unique qualifications. And, like the President, he possessed the ability to put his ideas on paper. Kissinger went to the White House.

He became a Kennedy brown-bagger. His job was to advise on nuclear weapons, and their effect on the politics of power. During these once-a-week visits, he would set about earning the reputation that hadn't caught up with him then— Super-stud! His colleagues still marvel at Kissinger's uncanny ability to dedicate his energies totally to the most complex of intellectual dilemmas—and then to match that dedication with a compulsive social life.

In the years that followed before his Nixon association, Henry Kissinger and I met a number of times. Although I was impressed by his ability, I would not in that era have anticipated that he would become the second most powerful man in the United States government. (And, indeed, he is much more than that.) He made some speeches and wrote some books. They were studied, applauded, and shelved. He and President Kennedy eventually parted ways, for reasons I'll detail later.

I went West to teach law. Kissinger went back to Harvard. But he's no man for an ivory tower, and by and by he attached his allegiance to Nelson Rockefeller. In the 1968 jockeying for the Presidential nomination, Kissinger fought against Nixon's nomination. He told New York radio host Casper Citron in an in-depth interview before the GOP nominated Nixon that, "Rockefeller is the only candidate at this time who could unite the country, who could appeal to Democrats and Independents with a program that could look to the future and focus America on its purposes."

Moreover, Kissinger had "grave doubts," he told Citron, "that Nixon can bridge the gap. . . ."

But after Nelson Rockefeller's Presidential prospects were jettisoned by Nixon and the men he hired to sell a President, Kissinger decided he'd rather switch than fight. He became a full-time house man for Nixon. The rest is history. Maybe he summed up the bliss of his conversion when he told a Nixon re-election rally, "Try it . . . you'll like it!"

I was lecturing in Constitutional Law when I read that Henry Kissinger had moved into the White House basement. Like many Washington-watchers, I had mixed emotions. Either Kissinger's joining Nixon was a total cop-out, or there was hope that the Millard Fillmore of the seventies had a chance. The Harvard types knew that Kissinger had the rugged determination to dominate the people he worked with. But Nixon had proved he was tough to handle. So I studied with interest the gradual power accretion of the President's aide—a climb at the expense of the Secretaries of State and Defense.

Within weeks after Kissinger joined the man he had tried

11

so hard to stop, most of the Professor's writings were Nixon-ized without so much as a changed comma. Even the plan for a China trip and shifting the Communist power balance was revitalized by Kissinger. (He had previously outlined it for Candidate Rockefeller, who had given it his approval, but never had the opportunity to effect it.) His power and influence in the White House became staggering.

Right at the outset when Nixon took office, almost everyone sensed that Kissinger was a unique addition to the Presidential family. I determined to find out what was behind the Professor's dramatic changes in affiliations—both professional and personal. I searched for the man.

I had some special qualifications for understanding him. My background, like his, included a stint in academic as well as political circles. While Kissinger was writing books and advising Presidents, I had become an international lawyer and successfully challenged Fidel Castro in our courts. Armed with a court order, I had attached Fidel's jet when he visited the United Nations. Then I had taught, lectured, and published at several colleges. My words were enshrined in the *Syracuse Law Journal* and the *Utah Law Journal* and no less an academic showcase than *Woman's World*. I wrote the biography of Angela Davis.

I became Law School Dean at a small California college. While there, I became associated with America's most gregariously successful lawyer, Melvin Belli, and learned that the rule book doesn't always work.

This chronicle wouldn't have been possible without the Hollywood syndrome known in the forties as "Kiss and Tell"; in the fifties as "How did you make out?"; in the sixties as "Did you score?"; and in the seventies as "Who is she as good as?" If anything, women were better sources of highly personal information than men. One interesting aspect of the Sexual Revolution is that Today's Woman loves to discuss the attributes of famous lovers with the same clinical candor her grandmother applied to infants' feeding habits.

I was assisted in my research by the loquacity of Kissinger's former aides, a retired Air Force General, two ex-White House secretaries, the Principal of George Washington High School, numerous Harvard competitors of Professor Kissinger, the headwaiter at Chasen's, two Parisian bell captains, one Las Vegas dancer, the files of a major news magazine, two West Coast daily newspapers, and little old lady librarians in two countries.

The reports on Kissinger's private life are the product of many interviews and press releases.

I found that his family life has been a well-guarded secret. I went to Germany to visit the town where he had spent the first fourteen years of his life in the era from Hitler's Beer Hall Putsch to his invasion of Austria and Czechoslovakia. I sifted through and discarded all sorts of publicity gimmicks to authenticate the actual facts of his later years.

It was one of his regular Washington dates who dubbed him "Super-Kraut." She says, "Henry is too busy for marriage but never too busy for sex." It was a complicated though pleasant chore to trace down the women he has dated in the Presidential years and separate the one-night stands from the ones that counted (and still count). Almost every available Hollywood beauty wanted to be included as one of Henry's girls. Only a few really were.

After following the trail of Henry Kissinger from bargaining table to bedroom and back again, I am convinced that this story should be shared with the world. Henry Kissinger is one of the most fascinating and powerful men on this troubled planet. It is much more than just a poignant, chilling joke when a night-club comic quips: "Remember! If anything should happen to Kissinger, then Nixon would be President."

So . . . armed with the sure knowledge of their implications for History, let's get on with *The Adventures of Super-Kraut.*

CHAPTER 1

———— ✠ ————

DR. STRANGELOVE

Note: For a world alerted to future shock, Consciousness I through III, and massaging mediums, there is a perilously fine line between fact and fantasy.

In the interest of truth and clarity, let me make one thing perfectly clear. There were a few occasions in this book when I felt compelled to indulge in fantasy. I found myself speculating on Kissingerisms that were never reported. When this was done, I have said so. All else is sober truth.

Following are two fantasies I have about the life of Presidential Adviser Kissinger. I shall leave it to you to judge how nearly fantasy follows fact.

K   *Good morning, Mr. President.*

N   *GOOD MORNING, HENRY. DO YOU HAVE THE SECRET REPORT READY FOR THE CABINET?*

K   *Not really . . . I went out last night and got in very late.*

N   *HENRY, LET ME MAKE THIS PERFECTLY CLEAR. I AM THE PRESIDENT . . . AND YOU ARE MY ADVISER. I HAVE NEVER INTERFERED WITH YOUR PERSONAL LIFE ALTHOUGH, GOODNESS GRACIOUS, I DON'T UNDERSTAND IT, PAT DOESN'T UNDERSTAND IT, JULIE DOESN'T UNDERSTAND*

15

*IT, AND DAVID CERTAINLY DOESN'T UNDER-
STAND IT. I DIDN'T MIND TOO MUCH WHEN
YOU WERE NAMED WASHINGTON'S CHERRY
BLOSSOMER. I DIDN'T COMPLAIN WHEN THEY
FOUND YOUR BEEPER BACKSTAGE AT CAESAR'S
PALACE. BUT THIS IS TOO MUCH . . . TOO
MUCH.*

K   *I'm sorry, Mr. President, but I met this unbelievable redhead
here for a silicone convention . . . she was truly unbelievable.*

N   *VERY WELL, HENRY, I WILL WAIT ANOTHER
DAY!*

K   *Thank you, Mr. President.*

N   *ALL RIGHT, HENRY, BUT DON'T LET IT HAPPEN
AGAIN. . . . .
BY THE WAY, HOW WAS SHE? . . . . .*

Fantasy No. 2

Realizing that an officer's duties do not include noticing a superior's bad breath, red eyes, or unpolished brass, the contingent of
Captains and Commanders that guard the White House Situation
Room manage to avoid seeing, hearing, or remembering the indis-
cretions of staff Generals and Admirals and especially their civilian
chiefs.

This being so, no one mentioned Mr. Kissinger's absence that
day from his post as National Security Council head and nuclear
button boss. He was not missed in the sub-basement of the White
House.

At 1800 hours West Berlin time on March 20, the Chief of
American Forces in Germany transmitted a top-secret, coded message marked FOR THE PRESIDENT'S EYES ONLY. The ur-
gent communiqué confirmed that the Russians had suddenly moved
up seven complete artillery and infantry units with rocket-bearing
tanks to a desolate sector of the Berlin Wall. It could have been a di-
versionary tactic. It also could have been a prelude to a sneak attack,
the closing of the Berlin Wall, and World War III.

The message lay undecoded, unprocessed, and unread for twelve hours. Nixon was greeting leaders of the Easter Seal Drive. His right-hand man was unavailable. Kissinger was getting laid!

The President's Chief Adviser on everything often engages in daytime sexual athletics. Fortunately, the delay occasioned by that day's acrobatic challenge did not unbalance the world balance of power. The Russian maneuver was just a drill. Kissinger's being incommunicado was not an isolated instance of man and power gone limp. It would do little more than raise the vicarious curiosity of the President. Its singular significance lay only in its selection as a fictional prologue to the true but fictionlike story of Professor Henry Alfred Kissinger. It was, in truth, only a fantasy—though a fantasy that was too close for comfort to reality.

Beginning of Sober Fact

When Henry A. Kissinger was appointed as the President's one-man brain trust, he entertained the cocktail circuit by impersonating Dr. Strangelove. Like the Stanley Kubrick movie hero, Kissinger is a nuclear expert with a German accent. He wields something of the same awesome power in the inner sanctums of government. The Kissinger story is far more Horatio Alger than Alger Hiss. It is a fascinating volume in a history being penned by a handful of men of America in the seventies and thereafter (if there be a thereafter). This man whose idol is not the conventional politician's Washington, Lincoln, or even Eisenhower—but the Teutonic Otto von Bismarck—has become the last and often the only voice the President hears and heeds. Who and what and why and how Strangelovian is Henry Kissinger?

Dr. Strangelove showed the world that a corruptive and corrosive power could exist and be nurtured by a nation's apathy. Henry's critics are only slightly more subtle. Others in Harvard's Government Department told *Time* they remember

17

him as an "uptight, fat, floppy, Teutonic professor." (He has lost some weight and relaxed a little since his Harvard days.) Administration critics sketch him as a power-mad man basking in the limelight that comes of being the second most powerful man in the first most powerful nation. His ironic propensity for Germanism has caused some of his Jewish contemporaries to suggest he is overcompensating for his family losses during the Nazi terror.

Placed in historical perspective, these criticisms seem overly dramatic. The head of state and his entourage are traditionally not great men. They are usually fairly glib guys with some pretty good ideas and the luck to be in the right place at the right time. The game of what would have happened if Dwight D. Eisenhower had lost the 1952 Republican nomination to Robert A. Taft, or if Adlai Stevenson had won, or even if the House of Representatives had broken the deadlock in 1800 by making Aaron Burr President instead of Thomas Jefferson, has made "hysterians" of historians for decades.

Today in living color, the electorate is beginning to realize that the labeling, packaging, promoting, and selling of Presidents and their decisions are little different from deodorant competition. (If yours doesn't work, fire yours. Hire ours.)

The ordinariness of men being the case, history must be reexamined. Grade school textbooks don't mention George Washington's padding of expense accounts (feeding one Army—$80,000). Children aren't advised that Benjamin Franklin had late-hour lady guests before orgies were fashionable in our nation's capital. The Blacks are quite right when they charge today that many of the men who drew up and adopted the Constitution of the United States were slaveholders.

One should remember that those who forged our nation,

with freedom of speech, assembly, and worship for all, included in that forgery their personal freedom to retain wealth, slaves, and power.

You must rinse out the brainwashing and appreciate the achievements of our forefathers, without begrudging them a little fourflushing. Then you can certainly accept a Nixon, whether you would buy his used cars or not. With every head of state you get many strange-loves, but the most intriguing of our time is the owlish, demanding, feared, respected, soft-spoken, dynamic, and surprising Henry Kissinger. After all, anyone who can reach the peaks of the China Wall and Jill St. John can't be all bad!

Most Jewish teen-agers who escaped from Nazi Germany were bowed in head and spirit—plagued with nightmares that left them sensitive and determined to avoid violence at any cost. A few like Kissinger seemed to develop an insulation of detachment and a second coat of arrogance. An aide like that is as valuable to a politician as a good-looking wife.

Titles are misleading in every field, but nowhere does the label more totally hide the man than in the corridors of the White House. Neither Henry's commission as Special Assistant to the President for Foreign Affairs nor his title as head of the National Security Council really reveals his role. He is the inseparable mental babysitter for the President of the United States.

Kissinger is adviser, counselor, companion, apologist, buddy, and spokesman for Richard M. Nixon. Most chief executives agree with Harry Truman that the buck ends in their lap. One of the few ways of living with this knowledge is finding a guy who is trustworthy and knows more about the world than the President himself. Almost everyone recognizes Henry's intellectual superiority when ranked with his boss.

Even Kissinger's critics who speak of the "Teutonic plague" in the Administration will agree on that point.

Kissinger's lips are stiff, forming only a straight line or a laugh, with no smiles allowed in between. His moods are just as extreme and deliberate.

Henry's job is sinister, with an image of war rooms and sheathed world maps illuminated by radar blips. His German accent probably could have disappeared. He uses it after nearly thirty-five years in America just as one of his friends, Zsa Zsa Gabor, does. It makes him memorable.

Henry speaks of himself as a Cold War warrior and sometimes warns that "Eastern Europe is enslaved" and "China is lost" and "Communism presses aggressively on everyone's peripheries. . . ."

He is an impressive theoretician. John F. Kennedy read a book that Henry wrote in the early sixties called *The Necessity for Choice*. It helped convince the young President to triple American spending for nuclear weapons. Kennedy sent for Kissinger and offered him a semi-official, well-paying, once-a-week consultant's job. He accepted. When Kissinger tired of Kennedy, Kennedy was just as tired of Kissinger. There were no farewell speeches. Neither made a fuss or issued any statement. Kissinger simply stopped taking the train down from Cambridge.

The consensus in and out of Washington is that Henry's strength and weakness are his vanity. The highest praise he can give to anyone is self-comparison. He once described Elliot Richardson, then Undersecretary of State, by saying, "I consider him in every important respect as good a man as myself." (President Nixon subsequently appointed Richardson as Secretary of Health, Education, and Welfare.)

When the turned-on press quiz him about an evening on

the town with "that girl," or Jill St. John, or any other date, his reply is often, "She's a great fan of mine."

Kissinger is a divorcé. Since his divorce, he seems to be once again overcompensating—this time, for his earlier reputation as a super-square. Few have been able to determine how much is reputation and how much is action. The young Washington, D.C., stud corps traditionally chases everyone from Ambassadors' wives to visiting beauty queens. They have voted him "fastest gun in the East." When a Cabinet member inquired about the balance of time between Henry's White House duties and his career as a swinger, he proudly replied, "Eat your heart out." (Wouldn't Dr. Strangelove have been a more interesting character if some color had been added to his social life? Or if he had had a social life?)

It was the summer sneak trip to China in 1971 that made Kissinger a world figure. Parisian television carried a low-budget movie on a day in the life of the great man. It was filmed in his fashionable Washington apartment, where he seldom takes a meal. After all, Kissinger is the prize catch of the capital's social circle and likes to eat around.

A sweet young thing in Paris called a press conference after viewing the film. She produced trinkets and snapshots, blushes and baubles, and proclaimed she was Henry's private stock. The Professor blew his cool and told newsmen, "She's just a castrating female."

Generally, though, he doesn't appear very unhappy about media attention to the ladies he sees. More than once, his well-publicized amorous excursions have served as a cover for secret diplomatic excursions.

The trip to China made Kissingerisms fashionable. It also brought back horn-rims and public horniness.

A week after his prelude to the President's visit, China was

21

in. Girls were going from buckskin and cartridge belts to peasant pajamas and chopsticks. Even Mrs. Nixon put together a Chinese wardrobe. Lord and Taylor demoted Pucci and did their Fifth Avenue window in chinoiserie.

When the week that "changed the world" in late February, 1972, was over, two things were clear. Taiwan was dumped and Kissinger was solid. The American President and Chinese Premier asked Henry to announce their joint communiqué.

Kissinger's office is antiseptic. It has fresh clean white walls with very little ornament. The desks are bland government issue. The staff is well-polished wooden. The wall across from his chair looks like a Zenith Remote Control Center with everything from cassettes to direct-line phones linking the world. The security is unbelievable. More guards watch his office than our Apollo Satellites at Cape Kennedy.

Kissinger brought the starched German work spirit to the White House. He drives his staff into a seven-day work week, with the days often lasting well into the nights. He comforts himself with the fact that most of his aides are ten years younger and falling out before he does.

The first real casualty was his Chief of Staff, Lawrence Eagleburger, who transferred from the State Department. After a few months of Kissinger, he had a nervous breakdown. Since then, no fewer than fourteen have come and gone from key positions. Their memories range from bitter disgust at the warlord to a frustrated disbelief of his energy.

Unlike many that have made it, Kissinger dislikes reminiscing about his rags-to-riches life story. He constantly tries to suppress identification with either the German or Jewish minority. He fears it will intrude on his reputation as an objective adviser to The Man. He even avoids discussion of the Israel-Arab conflict, despite its longstanding priority.

22

But the nature of his job is to serve first as an inseparable crutch for the President. They are constantly together, spending a part of each work day closeted from the rest. When important announcements are made or journeys taken to foreign countries, Kissinger is there, either with the President or as an advance Ambassador without portfolio. He rents the villa next to the Western White House in San Clemente. He even pays part of the rent personally. He spends more time on Air Force One than Pat Nixon, according to its official flight log.

This is the Kissinger story—the story of an ordinary-looking genius who is controlling our destiny. Here is Henry the Professor, Henry the Power, and Kissinger the Man.

CHAPTER 2

✠

GERMANY

*"The extermination of the jews is not a necessary evil . . . . , it is just
necessary!"*

—ADOLF HITLER

When the Allies chose Nuremberg in 1945 as the trial
site for the Nazis charged with mass murder, they picked a
city with its own history of persecution. In the fourteenth century, Jews were not allowed within the city limits. They
formed small colonies along the Rednitz River. Five miles
from where American judges sat, the town of Fürth had been
founded by harassed Jewish farmers.

Fürth, the birthplace of Henry Kissinger, is 980 feet above
sea level, and the people cough a lot from the harsh damp
winds that rise from the Ludwig Canal. In 1618 the river
banks were stained deep red for miles from the blood of thousands killed. The Thirty Years' War destroyed the royal palace known as "The Fürth" and wiped the town from the map.

More than three hundred years later the ghastly red dye
reappeared. Adolf Hitler was in power. This time millions
would die.

Today it's quiet in Fürth. Everyone is aware of Henry
Kissinger. They know he is a German, and they are convinced

25

that he is the real power in America. No one speaks of him as a Jew. The local Nazis are a small, closely knit group that drinks together and speaks of German greatness. Only when sober arrogance gives way to drunken boasting do the familiar phrases sneak out. "German technical know-how and personal strength is the greatest force in Europe," a young man told me in 1972. The youth believed that once again a great German empire would be established to "help" lesser countries govern themselves.

The elders of the little city are sad. A few are Jews. They reach seventy or eighty and never lose that strange look of hurt and forgiveness. When you enter a Jewish home today— no matter how modern it is—the prayer shawl and Bible are in the dining room. There grandparents still pray for their lost generations, but they show no hate for their neighbors or their parents.

The city is Catholic and confused. The young people are fascinated by the courageous doctrines of the young American priests. The girls want the pill. The boys want out.

Like their Bavarian neighbors, the people are strong and healthy. Many of the men work for the mining companies producing gold leaf, aluminum, and bronze.

The major factory in Fürth produces children's toys. Most of them are trains, dolls, and hand games. Embarrassed local officials have stopped any production of children's machine guns, grenades, and pistols. The optical instruments used by large American companies are designed and forged in Fürth. When you walk along the river, the air smells of beer from the breweries that ring the town.

Heinz Alfred Kissinger (who later became Presidential adviser Henry A. Kissinger) was born in Fürth on May 27, 1923. Many there still remember that year. German unemployment was at its worst. The people were divided, as as-

sorted extremists variously urged a military takeover, social-
ized factories, and getting rid of the Jews. Friedrich Ebert was
President of Germany. The country was desperately trying to
solve its unemployment problem, and was battling ruinous
inflation. In the winter of 1971 I met a man of seventy-eight in
Fürth, who remembers that he got married in 1923, and that
was the year that runaway inflation drove thousands penniless
from their homes.

In that very year of Henry Kissinger's birth in 1923, Adolf
Hitler tried to take over the whole German government with
his infamous Beer Hall Putsch in Munich. He failed, and was
sentenced to five years in prison. After nine months in jail, he
was paroled. He had utilized his time behind bars to write
much of Volume I of *Mein Kampf*.

The economy improved. Doctor Hans Luther, the Finance
Minister and acclaimed economic genius of Central Europe,
was able to stabilize the mark and halt inflation by creating a
new government bank and encouraging the investment of outside capital.

During Kissinger's first six years on earth, Germany prospered. Ironically, the principal source of investment capital
was loans that poured in from the United States. In 1925 President Ebert died, and the Rightist parties combined to elect
Field Marshal Paul von Hindenburg. The smallest block of
votes went to the National Socialist Party (Nazis), and they
were as yet relatively ineffective.

The terror had not begun when Martin Buber emerged as
the leader of German Jewry. Still, every year from the time of
Heinz Kissinger's birth, Hitler had gained a little more power.
By the time Kissinger was in his elementary school years,
there was a wild-eyed anti-Semite ready to fight on every corner. Heinz was not much of an athlete. But he learned to fight
because he was a Jew. He learned to run because he was a Jew.

27

His younger brother might be able to bluff his way out, but invariably Heinz was beaten up by his classmates who were training for Hitler's Youth Movement.

Still in 1928, when Kissinger was five, the country was prosperous and the Nazis seemed a long way from gaining power. The fourteenth coalition government of the Weimar Republic was formed, and Hermann Müller became Chancellor.

Louis Kissinger was a quiet, sensitive man—a respected Studenrät (teacher) in a girls' high school. His wife, Paula, was a middle-class hausfrau who did the cooking and cleaning and looked after their two sons: Heinz, who became Henry, and Walter, who was one year younger. The family lived in a five-room flat filled with books. (It was not the Jews' religion that was a threat to Hitler, but their learning.) The Kissingers even enjoyed the luxury of a piano, which Heinz avoided practicing.

By the time Kissinger was seven, the country was in crisis. The German economy depended on prosperity in the United States and Europe. After the Wall Street crash in 1929, when breadlines were forming in the United States and poverty became a household word in middle-class neighborhoods, Germany collapsed. The Weimar Republic had counted on continuing foreign capital and trade, and the Depression in the United States and the whole Western world ruined the Weimar economy. The German people became frustrated and angry, willing to go along with any new leader who promised a better life.

The Nazi Party in 1930 was promising anything anybody wanted. In an election on September 14, they picked up 107 seats in the Congress. They won in Fürth.

The national government was shaky, Hitler picked up

strength among industrialists and businessmen as well as the ordinary people, and there were three different Chancellors in 1932.

Hell began on January 30, 1933, when Adolf Hitler was appointed Chancellor and his Nazi party took supreme power in Germany. Within ninety days Jewish shops were pillaged and the first concentration camps were opened. Germany began to prosper again. Hitler spent tremendous sums on re-armament, and people had jobs. He told the Germans to be proud of their Aryan superiority and promised them the world.

Hitler withdrew Germany from the League of Nations that year because, "The rest of the world cannot keep up with us." He set up a Ministry of Propaganda and Public Instruc-tion headed by Joseph Goebbels. That agency was the lever for the control of the media and the arts and eventually ignited the fires that burned the books and disgraced a people.

The Catholic clergy was prohibited from practicing in Third Reich politics, and unions were abolished. On February 27, 1933, the Reichstag was burned—almost certainly by the Nazis. They did not need or want a Congress any more. Hitler could do it all, cheered on by Goebbels, Göring, and Streicher. It was easy for Hitler to turn the German nation against the Jews. Two depressions after World War I had left the German spirit near ruin. People were terrified and ready victims for mass hypnosis. The Jew in Nazi ideology was the embodiment of the enemies of Germany, all rolled into one. He was the traitor and the Marxist and the capitalist and the pacifist. All of the little ten-year-old Jews like Henry Kis-singer were "debasers of the purity of the German race."

Hitler's first anti-Semitic mandates were issued as early as April of 1933—two months after the Reichstag fire. (After a few years he did not bother reducing the prejudice and violence to print.) That first order dismissed all Jews from public employment as policemen, teachers, army officers, court officers, or government clerks.

From 1933 to 1939, while the lot of the Kissinger family and all other Jews deteriorated, Hitler was busy. He was readying the extermination of six million Jews and Catholics, four million Poles, and countless Czechs, Austrians, and Yugoslavs. He confiscated nine billion dollars' worth of Jewish property and plundered 400,000 Jewish businesses, ranging from giant factories to little shops. Jewish cultural and welfare institutions were pillaged. Schools were shut down. Teachers like Louis Kissinger first found it difficult to find work and then impossible. In 1935 the Nuremburg laws reduced all Jews to second-class citizens and prohibited inter-marriage with non-Jews. And then came 1938. This was the year when the world would no longer doubt Adolf Hitler's motives. Even the naïve and idealistic would see the brutal prophecy: Nazism would grow like a cancer in Europe and infect the world until it was cut out.

Orders were issued that year to destroy every synagogue in Germany, and more than 35,000 Jews were put in concentration camps in less than a month. Hitler was delighted. Not only were the Jews' factories and businesses providing money for his Party, but anti-Semitism was to be his wedge into the rest of Europe and the Americas. All money or property over $2,000 in Jewish hands became property of the state, and finally Jews were thrown out of all schools.

Well before matters had reached that point, Louis Kissinger was dismissed from his teaching job in 1933, and Heinz was expelled from his regular Gymnasium (a classical school for college preparation) and made to go to an all-Jewish school.

Heinz continued to avoid the piano. He preferred soccer,

where, mixed with a team, his personal lack of athletic skill wouldn't be noticed.

It is difficult to say how profoundly the Nazi terror affected Heinz. His older friends cannot erase from their minds the disgusting images that having lived an adult life under Nazism calls up. They insist that the key to his character lies in the cruel and humiliating loss of freedoms he suffered while he was growing up.

But Henry Kissinger says emphatically, "That part of my childhood is not a key to anything. I was not consciously unhappy. I was not so acutely aware of what was going on. For children, those things are not that serious. It is fashionable now to explain everything psychoanalytically, but let me tell you the political persecutions of my childhood are not what control my life."

His friends disagree. Twelve of his relatives died at the hands of the Nazis before Henry was fourteen. His father, who had lost his spirit when he lost his job as a teacher, thought the insanity might pass and he tried to wait it out. Mrs. Kissinger always took the lead in major family decisions; Louis was too busy with his books and dreaming. Finally the pressure became too much, and Paula persuaded him to leave Germany. Concerned for their children's education and the family's survival, they went to London in 1938, just before it was too late. There, an aunt helped them to arrange passage for New York.

Louis Kissinger did not have an easy time in New York. Coming to America was a reluctant chore and not a blessed exodus. He missed his teaching and his home. It was Paula who supported the family as a cook for neighbors in the East Side of New York when Louis found out that his German teaching credentials were of no value to him in the new world.

31

He was a deeply religious scholar, but his academic abilities were almost worthless to an immigrant with a wife and two sons in New York in 1938. Since he couldn't get a job in education, he took a clerical post in an upper West Side office. The family moved to Washington Heights. He continued in unskilled clerical work and spent years feeling frustrated and depressed. Even today his heart is in Fürth. Twice he has returned to visit, and he regularly writes to relatives and neighbors whom he remembers. He sends them articles about his Heinz from American publications and they mail articles about Henry from the German magazines. Now in his eighties, Louis Kissinger is thought of as a gentle, soft-spoken, soft-hearted man.

Paula Kissinger had always been a fine cook, so when she hired out for nice Jewish families on special occasions, her reputation spread. What had started as a neighborhood help-out grew to become a professional catering service handling bar mitzvahs, weddings, and even an occasional Gentile party. Paula still cooks for others, but she doesn't use her last name any more when she works because it embarrasses those who hire her. Henry was Honorary Chairman of New York's April in Paris Ball after he went to work in the White House, and that makes Mama "social."

Heinz changed his name to Henry and adapted brilliantly. In Germany he had been an average student. In Manhattan he became a straight A scholar at George Washington High School.

To push your way from immigrant status to a White House key office is a minor miracle. Kissinger developed a thick skin and learned to stand up to anti-Semitism on some days and anti-Germanism on others. His religion and nationality have always been made obvious by his speech, manner, and ideas.

32

Having survived Nazi Germany as a boy, Kissinger easily grew tough.

It is impossible not to speculate on how the many faces of Germany which Kissinger has seen in his lifetime have affected his personality and his policies. His adult feelings about his native country have appeared ambivalent. He tries to suppress any public identification with German or Jewish causes, but he is obviously more deeply concerned about Germany than about other foreign countries. He followed the statistics on successful Berlin Wall escapes fanatically. Yet he tells friends he fears another German "insanity."

He publicly revered *"Der Alte,"* Konrad Adenauer, who led West Germany to recovery as Chancellor from 1949 to 1963. Henry could be counted on as an ally for Adenauer's policies even when American officials disagreed. But he drew the line when modern German leaders began hinting for nuclear weapons.

His later writings show the effect of his German heritage and his Jewish fears. The result is his passion for international order. He pleads for the easing of tension—for a step back by all world powers. He dreams of a balance of power in which somehow "military bipolarity coexists with political multipolarity." The "SALT Treaty" signed in 1972 with the Russians is an example of Henry's handiwork.

Kissinger has no specific blueprints for peace, but he knows what must not be included. "H-bombs in Germany invite Hitlers," "Slave states must be freed," "Communist blackmail must not be tolerated" are the catch-all Kissingerisms by which he has risen.

Why does Kissinger think and act the way he does? It may be instructive to survey the many faces of Germany and their interaction with the United States that Henry Kissinger has seen in his lifetime.

When I visited Germany in 1972, I met in Hamburg a Jewish boy of thirteen who was preparing for his bar mitzvah. The news of the day was a scandal involving Economic Minister Karl Schiller, who had slipped his new wife's brother into a well-paid federal post. Vice-Chancellor Walter Scheel and Defense Minister Helmut Schmidt were trying to capitalize on it. Scheel was fairly loyal to Social Democratic Chancellor Willy Brandt, but Schmidt was interested in pushing his own Socialist Party so he might gain Willy's chair. Politics as usual, you might say.

Henry Kissinger's bar mitzvah and his country's government in 1936 were a totally different world. In the United States, a bar mitzvah is chopped liver, pen and pencil sets, and dancing. For that boy in Hamburg in today's Germany, it has become the same sort of thing. But in 1936 it was different, and religious Jews like Louis Kissinger taught their children Torah lessons secretly.

In 1936 Adolf Hitler had been Chancellor for three years, and he had assumed total dictatorial powers. Everything had to conform to Nazism, and Bavaria was a brutal police state. Already his objective of "Tomorrow the World" was being implemented with all sorts of secret strategies. In 1935, three years before the Kissingers escaped from Germany, while Henry was enjoying a quiet party with neighbors in his father's flat, Adolf Hitler and Admiral Wilhelm Franz Canaris were sharing a quiet supper and discussing espionage and Nazi intelligence in the United States. Canaris was the head of Abwehr, the German secret intelligence service. He did his job very, very well.

In 1938, 17,199 Germans left their country and arrived in the United States as immigrants. They were one-fourth of the total immigrant population of the year.

Roosevelt had defeated Alf Landon by a landslide election

in 1936, and Secretary of State Cordell Hull was trying to rebuild a world based on peace. A man who would be forgotten when he went out of office, James C. Dunn, was Roosevelt's key adviser on foreign affairs and political relations. This was the job that the fifteen-year-old immigrant boy, Henry Kissinger, would fill thirty years later.

In that year of 1938, France and Britain gave in and sacrificed Czechoslovakia to Hitler. Then Austria fell. Japan and China were at war, and world hell broke loose.

When the Kissingers became residents of New York State, the Governor was Herbert H. Lehman. On the day they arrived, Franklin Delano Roosevelt was on the radio urging Americans to throw out those in Congress who opposed the New Deal.

Hitler was preoccupied with the invasion of Russia and was not concerned with the United States. England was already appeasing the Führer, and Hitler did not think he needed spies there either. Canaris, who was to be revealed fifteen years later as the master spy of the war, disagreed. He believed an international network of top intelligence officers in every major nation was essential to Hitler's conquests. His principal target would be New York City.

When the Louis Kissinger family settled in New York, they lived less than a mile from a popular Rathskeller in the heart of Germantown. There were more Nazi spies in the United States that year than in any other country in the world except France. The beer halls on New York's East Side were hangouts for information sellers and passers. And anti-Semitism had crossed the Atlantic.

On February 27, 1938, Hitler's Foreign Minister Joachim von Ribbentrop learned in Berlin that FBI agents in New York had arrested Guenther Gustav Rumrich of the Denver Chemical Manufacturing Company. Postal authorities had be-

35

come suspicious over the large amount of German mail his girl friend was receiving at her Manhattan beauty salon. Thousands of surveillance hours later, the New York-based Nazi espionage team was broken up, and America moved closer to world war. In that atmosphere of fear and suspicion, a Jewish family moved into cramped quarters in New York City. The father was a teacher and the mother a good cook. There were two sons—Henry, who was almost fifteen, and Walter, who was a year younger.

In less than four years, the United States was at war with Germany and Japan.

It took years after World War II for the United States and Germany to become close allies. New generations of both nations put World War II next to the first one in their history texts, smiled, and went about their business. The Soviet Union and the Cold War were effective instruments to reconcile the United States and West Germany. In 1961, the East Germans erected the wall to thwart the Berlin airlift by Western allies. East Berliners were shot daily trying to escape to the West.

After fourteen years in power, a frustrated and tired Chancellor Adenauer retired and was succeeded by Ludwig Erhard, the German economic genius. He failed and was followed by Kurt Kiesinger. Kissinger liked him—he was tough. But Kiesinger's coalition government only lasted until early 1969, and then Willy Brandt became Chancellor a few months after Nixon became President and Kissinger became Presidential adviser.

The strongest factor in Germany's political life has always been its geography. It is the nucleus of Europe, and all trade must go through it. Since 1945 the nation has been the ouija board for American-Soviet relations. The two super powers have been poised and ready for years. Many experts believe that, if and when war happens again, it will start in Germany.

West Germany's population is more than three times that of
the East; it also controls coal, iron ore, and hydro power.

But all is not well in the country which boasts of having
Europe's lowest illiteracy rate. The Volkswagen may have
revolutionized the automobile industry, but there is no air of
confidence even in that business.

A trip to Germany today is bewildering. On the surface
there are industrial growth, political stability, and pride. But it
seems artificial, and it is. There is an undercurrent of confusion. France and England and the Scandinavian countries are
constantly urging Germany to think European. America, on
the other hand, is pressuring for a broader Atlantic concept.
Nazi is not such a bad word any more.

When he travels throughout Europe, Henry Kissinger reminds leaders of all countries that every German half a century old has survived three revolutions. Four different regimes
have taken control of that country—a country that lost two
world wars, suffered economic catastrophe, and yet survived.
Survival is the stuff that Germans are made of. Occasionally
prosperity creeps in. The standard of living in Berlin is about
that of Milwaukee or St. Louis. Perhaps our cities have a little
more desperate poverty.

The horrible ruins and the orphaned, starving waifs that
decorated the posters urging gifts for Europe are now largely
replaced in Germany by discotheques, topless joints, good restaurants, chic boutiques, and modern office buildings. There
are hardships, but they are not seen in the cities.

Yet the pressure is still there. Kissinger claims that Germany has suffered too many breaks in "historical continuity"
and too many shocks to sustain much pressure. The insecurity
is present everywhere. The top men in government look over
their shoulders at the young radicals who want to move them
out. Business leaders share the nightmare that once again Ger-

37

many will be isolated and confront hostility from its neighbors on all sides. When the college-age sons of the nation's leaders speak of Germany's power and superiority, the elders walk away. Then they shudder!

One of the high-ranking officials in the province where Henry Kissinger lived is a former Colonel in the Nazi Army. His job in 1943 was supervising the shipment of trainloads of Jews from Poland to concentration camps near Munich. Today he is a civil servant charged with administering health programs. His secretary is thirty-two and Jewish. Her father and two uncles died at Auschwitz.

Young Jewish people in Germany today follow Henry Kissinger's exploits with interest. He is a hero. Most of them have cast off the orthodoxy of their grandparents and the conservatism of their parents. They remain Jews and proud of it—but not religious.

In Fürth, where Henry and his brother were forced out of the Gymnasium, or German high school, because of their religion, prejudice is more subdued. The turning point was the economic crisis after World War II when Jews from throughout the industrial world responded and helped rebuild heavy industry in Frankfurt, Berlin, and Leipzig.

A shoemaker in Fürth remembers the underground meetings in his shop. After the war the black market dealers met in the same room. There were also Army crap games. In his desk is a scrapbook with headlines from a smuggled copy of the *London Times* showing Hitler's invasion of Poland. He also has the obituaries of most of his family, and a picture from an American newspaper of the son of a former customer, Louis Kissinger, a schoolteacher that he once knew. He, too, has survived.

The shoemaker is not surprised that Kissinger is important in the White House. "After all, Dr. von Braun is German and your best scientist . . . why shouldn't a German be in your White House?" He seems momentarily to forget that Kissinger is the aide and not the President, as Nixon has made perfectly clear.

The kids that played and studied and hid with Henry and Walter Kissinger in Germany are not all gone. One of them is Fritz Allman, whom I met when I was in Fürth. The parents of Fritz Allman escaped with their son and daughter in 1939 before it was too late. The elder Allman was a bookkeeper—but a Jewish bookkeeper—and his office was burned to the ground on June 3 of that year by the Nazis.

In 1955, when his mother died, Fritz took his father back to Bavaria. They wandered for weeks reminiscing and trying to find old friends or relatives. They couldn't. The father became ill, and Fritz took him to a modern German hospital in Franconia. He died there, but only after the valiant efforts of a young German doctor had failed. The doctor's father had been a Nazi officer. Patients were still asked their religion for the hospital chart, so the doctor knew his patient was Jewish. "I believe that he treated him as he would have his own father," Fritz swears.

More than fifteen years later, Fritz Allman is still in Germany. Now he exports toys from Fürth, and he goes bowling and he hunts. He, too, has survived.

Usually when a casual acquaintance becomes famous, we all tend to exaggerate or even invent a close friendship. Not so with Fritz Allman. He says he was rather friendly with Walter Kissinger, and he only vaguely recalls the brother Henry as a pretty good soccer player.

But he remembers 1938 well. Before his father's office was burned, the synagogue was ravaged by kids his own age readying for the Nazi youth camps. That night they left swastikas in front of all the homes of Jews in the province.

39

Allman is a member of the Christian Democratic Party, which pushed for pro-American policies in the new German Federal Republic. He did not like President Nixon at first, but he has changed his mind. Like many in Europe, he still fears the Russians, and thinks Nixon will stand up to them. "Kissinger is not really that pro-German, but he would not let us be destroyed," he says of his former schoolmate. Allman is proud of Germany today. He speaks of the tolerance and the peace and the opportunities. But he does not want his country to have nuclear weapons. Like Kissinger, he knows the tendency of many Germans to abuse power.

Allman thinks that Kissinger will last another year or two as a power in the White House and then disappear. "German Jews are very temperamental."

The German newspapers and magazines have made a legend of Henry Kissinger in his own time. While we see and read of the Presidential aide regularly in *Time* and *Newsweek* and lesser magazines, he is also a superstar in the German media. They had a field day when President Nixon revealed the secret Paris talks. They ran pictures of the home where the meetings were held, and maps showing the route that was taken when Kissinger landed in Europe. And they featured the "cover story" of Henry's Parisian rendezvous with CBS producer Margaret Osmer.

Since the Kaiser was first seen in public with a young prostitute, Germans have been relatively tolerant of public leaders' social life. Henry Kissinger is no exception. Our glamorous movie stars were once symbols of "American decadence." Today our best television shows are syndicated throughout Germany, and I saw long lines outside a theater showing *Midnight Cowboy* and a James Bond thriller. Germans are amused by Henry Kissinger's game of musical chairs with pretty women. A Berlin Film Festival official tried for three months to fix up the world's most famous bachelor with a well-stacked young protégé from Frankfurt, but Kissinger declined. He showed up at the event instead with Margaret Osmer, who was a good representative of this country, looking like a Doris Day movie extra.

Not many feet from the movie theater showing American films are some remnants of the bombings before U.S. troops occupied Fürth in the last year of World War II. Both the fourteenth-century church and the nineteenth-century City Hall in their Italian style still stand, making the city look a little out of place in central Bavaria. Most of the town was rebuilt, and at first it prospered, but then came inflation, depression, and inflation again, and the job was left unfinished.

One member of the faculty in a local school suggested that a monument might be set up in Fürth to Henry Kissinger for all that he has done for peace in the world. The local officials would not put up the money, so he went to private families soliciting funds. There is still no monument.

It is a 400-kilometer train ride from Fürth to Berlin, and you pass through Bamberg, Weimar, and Leipzig. These names first became widely known to the American public as bombing targets in 1944 when General Eisenhower was preparing for the Allied D-day invasion of western Europe on June 6, 1944. The people working on the train are that same sturdy brand that seem to work trains in every nation. They all know who Henry Kissinger is. In the cities, everyone speaks English. But on the train, the workers are older folks who cling to German with their provincial dialects. Most thought that Kissinger was the Foreign Minister. Some thought he was the Prime Minister. Others thought and knew the truth—that he was just the Secretary of State in the United States.

They know he came from Fürth and escaped from the

Nazis. Most remind you very quickly how the German people helped the Jews. It would seem as if everyone had helped write a *Diary of Anne Frank*, and the Nazis had no support.

The countryside of Leipzig might be Kansas. The farms are prospering, and the people friendly. Only among the students is there any tense radicalism. They are not satisfied with what Adenauer did, or with Willy Brandt. They think that their country is being exploited by America and England and France. They sound like German De Gaullists. When you ask them if they are Nazis, they say they are Germans. But many sound like Nazis. These people do not have one leader yet. They do have an idea—that Germany should be restored to its position as one of the great powers of the world with an Army and industrial base that is second to none. They do not talk in terms of conquest, but in terms of defending their existence, which they genuinely believe can be done only with might.

Article 20 of the basic law of the Federal Republic of Germany says that all Germans "shall have the right to resist any person or persons seeking to abolish their constitutional order, should no other remedy be possible." This is the keynote to the young German movement. The country is democratic and a social federal state, and supposedly all authority emanates from the people. Not all the people are satisfied with the rather slow pace that Germany has accepted in world competition.

The young German union leaders and professionals dislike what Kissinger and other Americans have admired most about Willy Brandt. They are bitter about his authoritarian style, which leaves little or no room for criticism or change. This does not shake Willy Brandt. He has the majority in the Bundestag and a supporter named Henry in the White House, and so the government has stayed together, though barely.

The country's most outstanding alumnus has found himself involved in the fight for survival by the Willy Brandt regime.

The social-liberal government has remained on the brink of collapse as a result of internal dissension. The progress that former Berlin Mayor Brandt promised and started has petered out.

Brandt went into office after Kissinger had been with Nixon only a few months. At first Willy's reform ideas clashed with Henry's advice to the President. After a lot of arguments on both sides of the Atlantic on German economic and foreign policy, it became apparent that Brandt was a winner. The Nixingers like to go with winners. Brandt picked up a Nobel Peace Prize in 1971 for trying to reconcile with the East, and so Kissinger supports him.

But the great domestic reforms that swept Brandt's Social Democrats into power are now drooping. Abortion law changes, modern divorce procedures, lower taxes, and broader education plans are bogged down in study groups or committees trying to find the financing for the idealism of Willy Brandt.

The personality clash between Brandt's most powerful minister, Karl Schiller, and his colleagues also threatens to overturn the government. In railroad stations, factories, coffee houses, and union meetings, Germans are taking sides. Despite all the rehabilitation since 1945, the country still leans on the United States to keep its economy fixed and its foreign position stable. Kissinger is expected to be a human gauge of public sentiment for Brandt, his ministers, and his policies.

A man who left Germany thirty-four years ago as a teenage Jewish refugee, escaping the barbarism and genocide of Adolf Hitler, is now the key to American support for 79 million Germans, 51 percent of whom are Protestant and 46 percent of whom are Catholic. The country has dropped the first two stanzas of "Deutschland," and the national anthem is just the third verse beginning, "Unity and justice and freedom."

43

CHAPTER 3

✠

THE BROTHERS

Kissinger's kid brother has become a quiet millionaire. In his late forties (one year younger than Henry), Walter Bernhard Kissinger is President of Allen Electric and Equipment Company in upstate New York. Henry says his brother is "the charming Kissinger." Walter's former associates say he's a "ruthless fanatic."

Presidential Aide Kissinger has acquired more power than all Americans but one in his soar to White House fame. Industrialist Kissinger has acquired more wealth than most in his business takeovers during the same years.

Walter keeps in better shape than his brother, the Professor. He's better looking, does not wear glasses, and his jokes are not as dry. "I think you have a brother working for the government," a visitor once told Walter. "You mean he has a brother working here," he replied. Secretly, he feels the press has paid too much attention to his older brother. He would like headlines for his own success story.

Executive Kissinger is a fascinating powerhouse of a man whose office shows the mementos of business hunts and a tiger skin or two.

45

"As kids we were two rivals," he remembers, "but there was no great competitiveness in our relationship. We're different men with different careers."

Five years after they arrived in America, Henry and Walter were inducted in the U.S. Army. Ever since that time they have gone in different directions. Walter was sent to fight the Japanese and advanced from Private to Lieutenant on Okinawa. After that, it was Korea and the rehabilitation of industry. The Japanese had disappeared, and the factories had to be reopened or the people of Korea could not survive. So Walter went from infantryman to mining executive as he tried, at twenty-one or so, to get the coal industry rejuvenated. Koreans were freezing, and his job was important. He did it well.

Henry's military career led him back to Europe, where his record of accomplishments during the American Occupation was no less phenomenal than his brother's in Asia.

After his discharge, Walter stayed in Korea as a War Department consultant. In 1947 he came home to go to Princeton. He was graduated when the late Senator Joe McCarthy was pursuing Communists and scaring intellectuals out of government. At first the bright young men from Harvard, Yale, Princeton, and the rest planned to do battle and help the country realize that McCarthyism was just one degree short of Fascism. Only a small group of Princeton graduates went to Washington to make noise and raise hell against the censured Senator. Walter was not among them. Like most of his classmates, his interest in public service became deflected.

He applied to law school and was accepted by both Harvard and Yale. Then he turned them down and chose Harvard's Business School instead. Although Walter had topped his older brother scholastically in Germany, Henry caught up and surpassed him in America. Walter never could muster the devout concentration that Henry showed in every subject.

For many years, Papa Kissinger longed to return to his school and friends in Bavaria, but he found genuine joy in his sons' academic achievements. Walter earned his share of extra-curricular honors, and next went the normal Harvard route to a multimillion-dollar corporation.

A small electronics firm, Advanced Vacuum Corporation, looking for a bright executive who knew marketing and the economics of production, recognized Walter Kissinger. "They offered me a small part of nothing. The company had a negative net worth, it was valueless, and I took the gamble," he says. When Kissinger took over, the company's sales were $50,000 annually. Walter dug in, trimmed expenses, pressured his colleagues. Four years later sales were over $2 million.

This was the era of the charismatic public issue and the merger. Walter found a similar company and, realizing the public would buy the glamour of electronics, worked out a combination which one year later sold over $10 million of the same product other companies were dying with. Then Kissinger bailed out and took his stock with him. He found another hungry company and pushed it from red to black while pushing his personal reputation even higher.

By 1968, when Henry was trying to stop Nixon from stopping Rockefeller, Walter had become a millionaire several times over. (Zsa Zsa, you got the wrong Kissinger!)

"My main interest is not making money, but in building an organization," Walter claims. He moved in and out of several other companies before settling down at Allen Electronics.

The Allen Company was like many glamorous electronics-age firms whose stocks jumped high and then plunged to the bottom. Kissinger came in as a combination efficiency expert and troubleshooter. He plays rough. He immediately sold off several subdivisions and reorganized their national organization. Allen is a manufacturer of automotive test equipment,

47

radiators, and car-wash facilities. There must be some very clean cars in the Kissinger garage—as 1971 sales reached over $123 million.

Walter, like Henry, needs a team of personally dedicated aides. His executive turnover at a corporation is comparable to Henry's casualty list at the National Security Council. He never hesitates to bring in new executives to implement the Kissinger method of moneymaking.

Walter earned his half of the family's reputation for ruthlessness when a California subsidiary's auto computer research project went sour. One former employee remembers Kissinger's rage when he arrived at the West Coast branch to find out what was going wrong. The firm had spent $6 million on a diagnostic computer to spot problems with car engines. "It was a bust. . . . The company's cash position was threatened." Walter moved as swiftly as Henry has been known to in crises and within a week the payroll was cut in half. He had fired half of the subsidiary's employees on the spot.

Both Kissingers accept authority and could stay in Harry Truman's kitchen without fear of getting burned. Walter is louder, and his forcefulness more obvious. But Henry's executive decisions are as firm at the White House as his kid brother's in the board room.

Overcompensation is a natural Kissinger tendency: Henry was the straight guy who, after divorce, had to be seen with every available swinging chick. Walter did his stint at overcompensating by easing Allen out of government contracts after he took over. He foresaw that, with the immense power Henry Kissinger has grabbed, critics would look for vicuña coats and favoritism first in his brother's companies. Not so, says Walter, who insists he has not benefited from big brother's big job, and he claims he has leaned over backward to keep his company from doing business with the government, so no one could make the charge stick.

It wouldn't be America if one who is related to a Washington big shot wasn't hassled for personal favors—the non-profit kind. Since Henry went to the White House, Walter has been besieged with invitations to social and civic events in the hope his brother might come along. Many wanting White House help on a pet project assume they have a potential sucker and ally in Walter Kissinger. To illustrate: The New York Zoological Society was pushing for President Nixon to squeeze time into his China talks to lay groundwork for a panda expedition to prevent the rare animals' extinction, and sought Walter's help. He demurred, feeling Nixon was more concerned with the potential extinction of mankind. Even though Walter considers himself a naturalist and was sympathetic, the plea never reached Henry.

Henry retains the seedy, smoky look of the all-night office man, who darts out for quickies at mealtime. Brother Walter is healthier and spends considerable time riding, hunting, and mountaineering. His family of six are regular campers and listen to Henry's adventures by transistor under Montana mountain skies.

The Kissingers have stayed close. Henry's divorce in 1964 had little effect upon the regular visits among cousins and with Uncle Walter. Despite the awesome power which Henry wields, he is still able to relate to the brother who shared an escape from the Nazis and went on to his own conquests. Walter is a frequent Washington visitor, and brings Henry's kids and his own to the White House basement.

There is only one year's difference in age, and both are men of genius level. But there is one big distinction. Walter's financial success and outdoor life have given him a relaxed, confident air. When he is arrogant, it's deliberate and controlled. Henry has that strained, taut air of a man whose every move and every word affects mankind, and if he goofs . . .

The woman least spoken about in everything written regarding Henry Kissinger is his ex-wife, Ann Fleicher. She, too, is a refugee and dated Henry for nearly seven years before they were married in 1949. They had met when both worked nights addressing envelopes. And Ann had kept on working to help finance Henry's years as a Harvard student. The Kissingers got divorced after fifteen years of what she claimed was a totally "unhappy marriage." She told friends that Henry was impossible when he was working on a research project that would later produce a book. When he returned home at night he would be so busy contemplating his next day's work that he would forbid his wife or anyone else in the house to talk. It was a mechanical existence.

Actually, Henry's ex is friendlier with his younger brother Walter than she is with Henry. They go through the motions of friendship, as so many divorced couples do, so that the children do not see any unpleasantries when they visit their father in Washington.

Daughter Elizabeth is twelve and considered the more intelligent of the two Kissinger kids. Her younger brother David looks a great deal like his father, except for the blond curly locks. He is a talented, self-assured lad. One of Kissinger's aides, David Halperin, remembers an incident when young David was with his father on a White House plane. "David was drawing a picture," Halperin recalls. "One of the White House wives looked at the drawing for a minute and said, 'Why, that looks like a drawing of you, David.'

" 'It is,' David said.

" 'In fact, it looks like a Michelangelo self-portrait,' she said.

50

" 'No, it's not at all in the style of a self-portrait by Michelangelo,' David responded very thoughtfully and seriously. 'I think it is in the style of a Raphael portrait of Michelangelo that I once saw.' "

It was the same outspoken young ten-year-old who tipped the world about President Nixon's departure date for China and brought about embarrassed denials by the White House press secretary weeks before the official announcement was made.

David was born when Henry had achieved his full professorship in the Government Department of Harvard University. Only two years later, after his concentrated work in the Department and in publishing, the Kissingers were divorced.

Now Henry works hard at his bachelorhood. In his elegant rented townhouse not far from Rock Creek Park, he has a maid who does a little housecleaning, but never finds dirty dishes in the kitchen. He is not around enough to eat at home. He sleeps there and shaves, and then splits. Very few people can claim to have been entertained in the Kissinger apartment. When he does decide to have a party, others handle it for him.

The Kissinger social life is centered on official White House functions and West Coast rendezvous with his contingent of lady friends. He keeps several of those little folding toothbrush sets handy for overnight trips.

But there is almost always time for a phone call to his brother, his mother, or the kids. All have been guests of the Nixons at one time or another, and have even received a Presidential Yom Kippur greeting.

CHAPTER 4

✠

THE JEWISH PRIVATE

The United States Army has generally enjoyed an international reputation as a great, spirited fighting force. Domestically its reputation is somewhat different. Ex-GI's of every rank, size, and era can attest to the "Flickett Syndrome" as an uncontrollable factor in Army personnel policies. Orville Flickett was a Corporal with a sixth-grade southern education and no experience in office matters. His first assignment was in 1945 as a clerk in a counterintelligence unit at Camp Gordon, Georgia, when German prisoners were kept there.

Next, he moved to the Communications Headquarters as an "intelligence analyst" specializing in breaking enemy code signals in South Carolina. Not bad for a guy who didn't even speak good English, let alone a foreign tongue. Flickett's name kept appearing on rosters listing his previous jobs. Each reviewing officer would assume he was qualified because of past service. As if in some nightmarish offshoot of the Peter Principle, Flickett was promoted, decorated, and transferred repeatedly. He ended up at the Pentagon in the cryptography center. It is reported that he tripped while entering the men's room at the Pentagon gym one day, broke an ankle, and was discharged with thanks by a grateful government.

The Army has tried to minimize incidents showing the

Flickett Syndrome. IQ, personality, and vocational aptitude tests are given each new recruit, and a team of psychologists study the results before feeding the new soldier's qualities into a computer for assignment.

Yet, despite all these innovations and the millions spent on modernizing the service, you can still find a master mechanic slinging hash. And back in the pre-computer era of World War II, it happened more often than not.

Being drafted brought good luck and bad luck to Henry Kissinger. In the second week of basic training he (along with a few hundred other GI's from the New York-New Jersey area) was given a battery of tests. Among them was a standard IQ measurement, through which Army personnel discovered they had a genius on their hands. A couple of far-sighted Generals had decided to bring together all the top brains among enlisted men just in case, sometime later in the war, their minds could be put to good use. It was an uncommon stroke of fine planning for the Army. About three thousand or so highly intelligent men were put together in one category to finish their education and be ready to serve. But then, having gone to such expense, the Army washed out the whole program. There had been opposition, charging that it was unfair to send stupid people to combat and keep brighter ones in college, even if they were needed.

This victory for egalitarianism was bad news for Private Henry Kissinger, and he was not happy as he neared the end of his basic training. Then one day a jeep roared up to his training post, and perhaps the gutsiest private in Army history jumped out demanding, "Who's in command here?"

Henry's Colonel came running out in front of the command tent and confronted this incredible buck private. "I am in charge here, Private," the Colonel said, not quite sure of himself.

54

The private yelled, "Sir, I am here at the General's order to tell your men why we are at war."

This ridiculous scene is deeply imbedded in Henry's memory, and it should be. What better example could there be of the Army's opportunities for a GI genius? It was not totally unknown for an enlisted man with a gift of gab to be used by his officers to give inspirational talks to his buddies rather than waste his talents on KP. The private in question was a thirty-five-year-old lawyer with a couple of Ph.D. degrees. His name was Kraemer. He had fled his native Prussia and was now going from camp to camp spieling the Allied concepts of World War II.

Kissinger was impressed and wrote a brief note, which struck Dr. Kraemer with its simplicity and sincerity. "Dear Private Kraemer," it said. "I heard you speak yesterday, and this is how it should be done. Can I help you? Private Kissinger."

Kraemer vividly remembers the meeting he arranged with Kissinger. It took him twenty minutes to realize he was talking to a man superior to himself in many ways, and another ten to conclude that Kissinger's was possibly one of the best minds for historical analysis he had yet encountered. This youthful Jewish refugee draftee had an incisive grasp of things around him and an intellectual cool that Kraemer envied.

Kissinger became Kraemer's protégé and was designated interpreter for the 84th Division if it should be sent to Germany. It was. Henry then became interpreter-aide for the Commanding General.

When the 84th Division occupied Krefeld, the city officials had vanished with the Nazi troops. They had been sympathizers of Hitler's regime, and were not going to chance the American Army's occupational policy toward pro-Nazi municipal leaders. There were a quarter of a million people wandering around, and they needed housing, clothing, food, health facilities, jobs, and supervision.

Dr. Kraemer somehow persuaded the Commanding General to allow Kissinger, still a private, to reorganize the government of Krefeld. He claimed he was qualified since he spoke German and had an extraordinary intelligence besides. When the under-twenty-five set are put down for lack of meaningful achievement by some of their elders, they ought to point to Kissinger's record in Germany. Within a week Krefeld had a functioning government, with Henry as its principal adviser.

"I could only marvel," Kraemer told the *New York Times* on November 14, 1971, "at the way this 19- or 20-year-old did the job. [Kissinger was actually twenty-two or so by then. —Author] Soon the government was again working in a splendid fashion. Henry had planned things wonderfully. This was a prodigy. He had a fabulous innate sense of finding his way out of the most difficult situations. Here this little Kissinger had set up in three days a working municipal government in a large city where everything had been run by the Nazis just two days before."

Kraemer raved to the General about Kissinger's accomplishments which made all the officers' jobs easier. The General raved to his colleagues, and a year later Private Kissinger was administering the entire German district of Bergstrasse. He did such a good job that he actually was given official authority to make unlimited arrests of German nationals for any reason he saw fit within the district. This was a weird kind of power to be thrust upon a draftee whose only apparent firsthand awareness of power had been gained watching the Nazi takeover in his native land when he was a youngster.

According to the Army, he never abused that power. He was given a castle of his own, but evidently that did not turn his head either. A couple of men in his unit remember he was cocky, but always willing to share the pleasant amenities he enjoyed as a combination buck private in Uncle Sam's Army and unofficial head of state in a German county. The people of Bergstrasse were grateful for his fairness and urged American officials not to transfer him out.

Private Kissinger became Sergeant Kissinger, and Private Kraemer became Lieutenant Kraemer. Henry's mentor had him transferred to the faculty of the European Command Intelligence school (where he met Private Flickett—a study in contrasts if ever there was one). Here they taught Allied officers how to find Nazis who were hiding in the community and taking refuge underground. Sergeant Kissinger's class consisted mostly of Colonels and Majors, and he was the best instructor they had. When his hitch ended, the Army hired him to stay on at the school as a civilian teacher at $10,000 a year. For an immigrant with no college education whose only other jobs had been working at a shaving brush factory and as a clerk, that was a fortune.

Lieutenant Kraemer had become a close friend. He was concerned that his protégé might be overwhelmed by all that money. But Kissinger was not, and he decided to go home. He told his friends, "I only know what I teach at the school. Otherwise I know nothing."

Kissinger did go home, and embarked on a course that would add to his personal worldliness. After Harvard as a student and Professor, and two Presidential preludes to his Nixon association, he no longer "knew nothing." His relationship with the military has also changed. Now, he has a Brigadier General as a personal aide, and the Joint Chiefs of Staff jump when he calls. In a figurative sense, he has become the only U.S. four-and-one-half-star General.

CHAPTER 5

————— ✠ —————

HARVARD AND WASHINGTON

After World War II, Kissinger had been determined to get a top education. He was encouraged by his family and friends, and was elated when he was admitted to Harvard.

He split his time between his major in Philosophy and his personal interest in the international political scene. He had already acquired the hard-line instincts which were to fuel him in later years for service in the White House. He had a natural insight into the historical processes that had brought the world to the power stand-off of the twentieth century. He reluctantly would accept an inevitable historic trend, but would still eagerly intervene in an effort to prevent the next decline.

When he was a student at Harvard, Henry was particularly impressed with the works of Oswald Spengler—especially his *Decline of the West.* Spengler's philosophy had an immeasurable impact on the young refugee student. One of Kissinger's closest colleagues, Stanley Hoffman, made the remark that Henry "walked, in a way, with the ghost of Spengler at his side."

At the end of his Harvard undergraduate work, Kissinger turned out a wordy 350-page thesis on the work of Spengler, Toynbee, and Kant.

Nobody but Henry Kissinger today would have the gall to

dream up a trip to Red China for the man who became President opposing Communism. No Presidential aide but Henry Kissinger today would have the audacity to be seen around town with various oversexed and underdressed starlets. His gall, gusto, and high-level theorizing started in school, as illustrated when he called that thesis *The Meaning of History*. It never reached the best-seller shelves and did not become required reading in any school systems. Its only real impact seems to have been an internal decision at Harvard that undergraduate students should not write so many pages on their senior theses.

In the part devoted to Spengler, Kissinger wrote, "Instinct is no guide to political conduct. Effective leadership is always forced—whatever its motives—to represent itself as the carrier of ideas embodying purposes. All truly great achievements in history resulted from the actualization of principles, not from the clever evaluation of political conditions."

From this, it seems that, even as a student, Kissinger subscribed to the philosophy he would later apply to the world scene with White House backing.

In the life that has been filled with unique achievements—from becoming supervisor of an entire district in occupied Germany while still a private, to serving as a Presidential aide of incomparable power—there are not many incidents like the one that occurred at Harvard which Kissinger does not like to talk about.

After he received his Ph.D. degree, it was assumed by the academic community that Henry would be appointed to the Harvard faculty. He had been a brilliant graduate student, and his writings had been good enough for some government officials to use. He was proposed for the faculty and was well-supported by some professors, but the decision went against him. It took two years for word to leak out that the adverse judgment had nothing to do with his academic credentials, but rather his attitude and the school administration's belief that Henry wanted a post on the Harvard faculty only as a stepping stone to better things.

The *Atlantic* Magazine revealed "details of the argument concerning Kissinger's appointment are an academic secret, but according to one of the reliable members of the faculty, he was judged a 'difficult colleague,' and he had the reputation of being nicer to his superiors than to his subordinates."

Now, although many of Harvard's top scholars do go on to guide government agencies and, indeed, reside in the White House, officially and publicly such jobhopping by faculty members is frowned upon. Supposedly, Harvard is above all that and offers its professorships only to those who sincerely want to gain tenure status and share their thoughts with generations of students.

Kissinger worked part-time at Harvard after that, but only on special programs and not as a full-fledged faculty member until much later. He was in demand for government projects.

There were other academic opportunities, of course. After the Harvard rebuff, the University of Chicago had rushed to offer Kissinger a full professorship, which they thought he would accept. (Another unwritten rule in top academic circles is not to offer the title of full professor unless you know in advance that the nominee will be delighted to have it.) After a good deal of thought, Kissinger turned it down. He decided it was too far from the Washington political scene, and that it would be better to stay with temporary employment at Harvard. Besides, he was holding out for the permanent professorship which had been denied him. He finally won, becoming Associate Professor of Government from 1959 to 1962, and Professor in 1962.

When Dwight D. Eisenhower was President, Kissinger

61

was asked to serve in a second-echelon job as a foreign policy strategist. He accepted, although he was not considered a loyal Republican and had no rapport with Eisenhower, either as a military strategist or as a politician.

When John F. Kennedy took office, Kissinger, like others at Harvard, was stimulated by the excitement of an intellectually permeated New Frontier. He had met JFK socially and liked him. With his connections and experience, Kissinger hoped to play a very important role in the new Administration. Arthur Schlesinger, Jr., who had been Henry's sponsor for some time and was one of JFK's advisers, recommended him to Kennedy. He was engaged as a part-time consultant, but there was no magic. Though Kissinger was impressed with Kennedy, the President told Pierre Salinger he found Henry's long-winded harangues "a little harassing." Upon realizing he was not being well received, Kissinger became critical of the Kennedys and started telling friends that he disliked the "rich boy" values of the Kennedy White House. In fact, Kissinger complained that there was no great sense of nobility or honor in the new Administration. After a short stint as a once-a-week consultant, he quit making the weekly trip from Cambridge. He was uncomfortable with the optimism of the New Frontier, and he disagreed with Kennedy's attitude toward the policies of France's President Charles de Gaulle.

Kissinger maintained his ties with Harvard and divided his time between research projects and political dabbling. He was a middle-of-the-road Democrat-Republican following men rather than political labels. The next President he worked for was Lyndon B. Johnson, who called on him for some special studies. The only important project undertaken for President Johnson by Kissinger was a trip he made to Vietnam with Clark Clifford, the man who in 1968 succeeded Robert S. McNamara as Johnson's Secretary of Defense. Indeed,

Clifford's name appears in most of the important political stories of the 1960's.

Johnson sent Clifford and Kissinger to Vietnam because he questioned the accuracy of the CIA's reports and wanted independent appraisals of American political policy there. Lawyer Clifford and Professor Kissinger were assigned to study the "political maturity and motivation" of the leaders of South Vietnam. They came to a simple conclusion: There was none.

Kissinger came back and told President Johnson that there was no real cohesive national government because the South Vietnamese did not have a good leader. The Kissinger study indicated that loyalty to family and clan among Vietnamese was far more important than any sense of responsibility to their country. Moreover, the government really represented only 15 percent of the people, and the other 85 percent, who were peasants, had very little voice in South Vietnam's affairs.

During the trip Kissinger listened to reports of waste of U.S. food supplies and technical assistance. There was a tremendous feeling that American aid officials were backtracking so they would not be called colonialists. In some cases, large quantities of foreign aid materials were sitting in warehouses, while the only supplies available were on the black market.

The guts of the problem was that the well-to-do Vietnamese (which included Army officers and government officials) had a discriminatory attitude toward the peasants. The peasant who went into the Army elevated himself slightly and enjoyed a bit of protection. But no help from the South Vietnamese government could be expected by the nonmilitary families who lived in the rural hamlets and might be blown up by Vietcong mines at any time.

As an instance of the Vietnamese government's indifference to the peasants, Kissinger and Clifford referred to the experiences of Dr. Howard Rusk, the specialist famed for his

63

work with the handicapped and disabled. President Johnson had sent Dr. Rusk to Vietnam to work on a program for the rehabilitation of paraplegic war victims. When he arrived, the Vietnamese government said, "Take care of our soldiers first." Those paraplegics who were civilians would have to wait. Rusk was incensed and made a symbolic gesture of having sixty paraplegics flown to New York for intensive treatment and rehabilitation, but none of the U.S. officials were willing to get tough enough with the Vietnamese government to insist that a representative group including peasants as well as soldiers should go to New York.

As a result of such episodes, it was not difficult to figure out why the resistance level among peasants was so low when the Vietcong came in. Kissinger and Clifford were bombarded with demands to change the American attitude to exert some pressure in remedying the shortcomings of the Vietnamese government. It seems to have been one of the few occasions when Henry spent most of his time listening.

What impact Kissinger's report had on Johnson is not clear. The only thing we know for sure is that it did not extricate Johnson from the morass of the Vietnam War and prevent the political disaster that resulted in Johnson's decision not to run for the Presidency again. Kissinger would assume a new role advising a new President. Only that damnable war seemed to remain the same.

CHAPTER 6

———————— ✠ ————————

BY HENRY KISSINGER

Henry Kissinger has always liked to write. He uses a lot of big words and does a very thorough job of explaining involved complications in international policy.

One of his books, *Nuclear Weapons and Foreign Policy*, originally published in 1958, became somewhat of a best-seller among those people who make a habit of studying American power strategy. The book grew out of Kissinger's work over two years with a group of experts that had been organized by the Council of Foreign Relations through Harvard. It talked about the development of nuclear weapons and the effect of these weapons on military strategy and foreign policy in the United States.

It received enthusiastic reviews from such publications as the *Political Science Quarterly* and the *Chicago Sunday Tribune*. "The modesty of Mr. Kissinger's title conceals both the magnitude of his effort and the depth and power of the analysis he has brought to it," said Walter Mills in *Political Science Quarterly*. Kissinger was attempting nothing less than a brand new theory of war and peace and inventing a unique international power relationship among great nations geared to meet their nuclear-weapon revolutions.

The man who has been unfortunately labeled the father of

the bomb, Edward Teller, wrote that the book would help teach a better way to contribute to the safety of the free world.

Although Kissinger's name was on the cover, the book certainly encompassed the work of many men. It included the best of the ideas of those who had been on the task force of experts convened by the Council of Foreign Relations.

The historian in Kissinger is most impressively revealed in another of his works. *A World Restored: Castlereagh, Metternich, and the Problems of Peace, 1812–1822* was a study of international politics and the attempts of a handful of European statesmen to bring about peace after the Napoleonic wars. Kissinger shows astonishing insight into the baffling incongruities of diplomatic tactics a century and a half ago. Understanding the power struggles that existed in the Napoleonic era is possibly a predicate for finding light among the crises of today. Reviews of his book were generally favorable, although no one commented on Kissinger's writing talent. The critics praised his research rather than his ability to put it down on paper. The *New York Herald Tribune Book Review* said: "Kissinger has good insights into the working of the international political systems we call the balance of power and the conditions under which it can maintain peace—or at least, absence of general wars." The reviewer observed that he exaggerated the merits of the diplomats he mentioned. Characterized as an interesting addition to the literature of an important era, the book was quickly shelved in universities in better public libraries, perhaps to be pulled out now and then by ambitious graduate students working on dissertations.

The little card that tells all in the back of the book I borrowed from the Los Angeles Public Library indicated that I was the second person in its fourteen-year history to borrow that particular copy.

In 1965, Kissinger edited a book of readings entitled *Prob-*

lems in National Security. The thick edition was a collection of about twenty-five excerpts from other books, articles, and speeches carefully catalogued under such headings as "Nature of Modern Power," "Strategic Doctrines in the United States," and "Alliances in the Nuclear Age." Kissinger's intellectual reputation enabled him to get permission from people like nuclear scientist Edward Teller and such members of the Kennedy and Johnson Administrations as Dean Rusk and Bob McNamara, together with their counterparts in Europe. This helped to justify the $8.50 cost for an anthology.

One magazine reviewer curtly summed it all up by saying: "Mr. Kissinger has issued a book and chosen the material fairly." This was certainly less enthusiasm than the accolades accorded *Nuclear Weapons and Foreign Policy*, and it never reached best-seller status, even on Harvard's campus.

In 1969 Kissinger's book *American Foreign Policy* was released, containing three of his previously published essays. The first one was important, and it took to task our whole domestic structure and the leadership styles of our past Presidents. It particularly emphasized their failure to understand the real problems of foreign policy. The second essay went into that policy itself and talked about the need for military bipolarity to coexist with political multipolarity. If you carefully examine the quotes in the second essay, you may discover that they seem to have reappeared in many of Mr. Nixon's speeches in the 1970's.

The third of his essays took on the Vietnam War, and suggested three levels of negotiations. Nothing was very new, but his presentation at least was fairly concise when he spoke in terms of the need of the United States to bring all nations to the bargaining table. Those who reviewed this book sensed Kissinger's tough-mindedness and the fact that he no longer harbored any illusions about judging our foreign policy by its goals rather than its deeds. Even though there was nothing innovative or surprising to be found, particularly when Kissinger described the postwar world, it was accepted as an important review for students. This essay was probably the most succinct work written by any scholar (or by the only scholar, depending on your point of view) in the Republican Administration of Richard M. Nixon.

Nixon was not the first President to use an eloquent staff member's publication as a test balloon for a new theory. This third essay was just such a feeler. Kissinger talked about the Vietnam negotiations, and his thoughts became the subject of discussions in the Congress as well as on many important campuses. Tremendous political interest was shown by major newspapers in the essay because it offered a shrewd appraisal of the issues likely to be raised in the negotiations, as well as some of the pitfalls. The *New York Times* suggested that Kissinger's book was being used to sound out the American people and prepare them for some of the very slow-moving achievements that the President ultimately hoped to reach.

A man is revealed fully in his writings—whether he likes it or not. The most interesting of Henry Kissinger's publications are his magazine articles. They display a toughness with respect to international power problems, but seem to be tempered according to his political mood. In 1959, he wrote in *Foreign Affairs* on a subject particularly sensitive to him. He spoke about German reunification and said that "to strive for German unification is not a bargaining device but the condition for European stability." This was one of the few times that Kissinger's appreciation of the German mind and manner, as well as his grasp of Germany's pivotal role in Europe, showed itself. As top aide to President Nixon, he has carefully avoided getting involved in the problems of either West Germany or Israel—to make sure he is never accused of having a vested interest. Kissinger suffers under a double handicap among those who fear Germanic power thrusts: His Germanism is obvious, and his Jewishness is neither obvious nor universally accepted.

In 1960—once again in *Foreign Affairs*—he wrote about "Arms Control, Inspection and Surprise Attack." Recognizing that there was no question that technology now enabled surprise attacks, Kissinger boldly wrote about what could be done in retaliation without ultimately destroying the world. He came to the elementary conclusion that the surest way to avoid surprise attack is to eliminate retaliatory forces by limiting nuclear weapons.

Back in 1962, the opinions in this country concerning the Cuban Revolution were not yet settled. Kissinger put together "Reflections on Cuba," and chose the academically important magazine, *The Reporter*, to publish it. It discussed the blunder that the Soviet Union had made concerning the Cuban missile crisis in 1962 and gave great insight into President Kennedy's handling of the showdown.

One of the quiet chapters in Kissinger's life is the story of his service as a one-day-a-week adviser to President John F. Kennedy. The late President didn't like Henry; but he respected him. They disagreed on Germany and Charles de Gaulle and a dozen other things, but Kennedy was not one to deprive the New Frontier of a brilliant man merely because he held a dissident position. Nor did Kissinger allow himself to be biased by Kennedy's dislike for him. His "Reflections on Cuba" registered his admiration for Kennedy's handling of the missile crisis.

In this article, Kissinger sternly took the Russians to task. He said that, if they had felt that missiles based in Cuba were necessary to an over-all strategic balance, then the Soviet arsenal of intercontinental rockets must be a lot smaller than the world believed. On the other hand, if the Soviets considered their arsenal of rockets adequate, then nuclear bases in Cuba were really irrelevant to any security problem. In plain language, Kissinger felt the Soviets had goofed. And probably he was right.

According to Kissinger's theory, Khrushchev had become convinced that the United States would never run risks to protect its interests. Khrushchev reasoned that the United States really doesn't understand its own interests, or is too involved politically to garner the necessary power to handle a real threat. "In the Suez crisis, we had collaborated with the Soviets and humiliated some of our closest allies. American intervention in Lebanon didn't prevent the displacement of the only Middle Eastern government that was going along with the Eisenhower doctrine," Kissinger observed in his Cuba article.

A year and a half before, the United States had gambled on direct intervention in Cuba with aid to the abortive rebel invasion of April 17, 1961, and totally accepted the failure when the Bay of Pigs disaster occurred. In Laos, America pretended to be ready to intervene but was quick to settle for a solution that was, at best, ambiguous. These were convincing illustrations to the Russians.

Kissinger reasoned that Khrushchev figured our soft reaction to the building of the Berlin Wall indicated a tendency on the part of the American government to accept just about anything that was *fait accompli*. All in all, the Soviet government seemed to subscribe to a formula that, if the United States government was given any face-saving option, it would choose retreat rather than a head-on confrontation.

When President Kennedy made it clear in a press conference on September 13, 1962, that he would take "a grave view of the introduction of offensive weapons in Cuba," the warning was so nebulous that the Russians were not deterred.

For a month or so, Kennedy's key advisers kept emphasizing the risks he would be taking by a blockade of Cuba or any invasion. They reminded the President that we had great intelligence about Cuban affairs and had seen no offensive build-up.

Then New York's Senator Kenneth Keating revealed a big build-up of offensive missiles in Cuba. The President's aides urged him to deny it. For the second time in his brief Administration, John F. Kennedy faced a grim crisis over Cuba.

Kissinger was right in saying that the Russians clearly misjudged the character of this particular President and the mood of the country. There was a desire for a New Frontier in the United States, but it could not be reached with weakness. The Soviets failed to understand that it is pretty unlikely for a man to be nominated and elected President of the United States in Kennedy's circumstances without a strong will and the guts to prevail. To become President he had had to overcome two major handicaps: his youth and his Catholicism. His whole personal history had prepared him for the crisis, and he was able to deal with it forcefully.

Kissinger greatly admired Kennedy's handling of the Cuban stand-off with the Soviets. He said: "The Administration demonstrated skill, daring, and decisiveness in dealing with the problem once it was recognized." But he expressed strong misgivings about the time required by the Kennedy Administration to assess the nature of the Soviet build-up. He saw that there was a policy question concerning the criteria of certainty upon which the American government would act. What would we do in the future? Would we have to wait

71

until we had "hard" intelligence about Soviet intentions, or could we come to a conclusion and move decisively? "The challenge is to couple up some prudence, decent calculation, and the skill of a government of experts" (which Kissinger favors over a one-man show) and "act with imagination," Kissinger said.

Years later Henry Kissinger would head up just such a team of experts and face his own crisis in Vietnam with even less public support than there was for the Cuban intervention.

The year after Kissinger wrote about Kennedy's handling of Cuba, he jumped literarily to another type of politician—Senator Barry Goldwater. Once again it was *The Reporter* that revealed Kissinger's reflections, in an article entitled "Goldwater and the Bomb: Wrong Questions, Wrong Answers." In this article he discussed the recommendations by Senator Goldwater that the President should inform the American people about all procedures for emergencies in the event of the President's death or disability. Goldwater was concerned about actual as opposed to theoretical Presidential control over nuclear weapons, if we ever got into a battlefield situation. He believed that authority should be delegated to the NATO commanders for the use of tactical nuclear weapons in certain circumstances.

Kissinger would never consider himself a Goldwater fan. But from this article and some of Henry's later statements, it becomes apparent that he had tremendous respect for the Arizona Senator's toughness. Although their backgrounds are so very different, with Goldwater a southwestern individualist and Kissinger an eastern-trained refugee, they do share the same value judgment on nuclear power and the control of it.

After the Goldwater article, Kissinger again wrote about German unity and the fact that the American people did not really understand French President Charles de Gaulle. In

Harper's Magazine in 1965 he focused on the dispute between the United States and France, pointing out the irony of the Franco-American rivalry in that, "De Gaulle had concepts that had gone beyond his strength, and the United States had strength that had gone beyond its concepts."

Many liberals were charging that De Gaulle was as dangerous as Hitler. Not so, said Henry Kissinger, who admired De Gaulle's take-charge attitude. This article subtly reflected Kissinger's differences with President Kennedy, who had been influenced by the Democrats in Congress opposing the Frenchman. Kissinger ultimately had given up his position as a White House adviser to the President over his convictions about French policy.

Neither Nixon nor Kissinger talk very much about Henry's position on Vietnam five years ago. It was in *Look* Magazine that he said any withdrawal would be disastrous.

The Harvard scholar earned his introduction to government power by putting in print precise concepts for politicians who couldn't be very precise. His articles have become an intellectual sounding board, with Presidential direction, seeking to soften the academic community to accept the Nixon policies.

Among Kissinger's other books used as reference works by various government agencies were *The Troubled Partnership*, a 1965 study of the Atlantic Alliance; *The Necessity for Choice*, a 1962 Doubleday book released for mass-market consumption, which sold poorly; and *Bureaucracy, Politics and Strategy*, published by the University of California just before Kissinger joined the Nixon Administration.

✠

CHAPTER 7

ROCKEFELLER THE LOSER

"When Nelson buys a Picasso, he does not hire four housepainters to improve it."

—HENRY KISSINGER (after he wrote a speech for Nelson Rockefeller which was rewritten by four of the Governor's regular speechwriters) as quoted by Patrick Anderson in the *New York Times Magazine,* June 1, 1969

Nelson Rockefeller has always surrounded himself with the best. He needs good people. Of all those bearing the illustrious Rockefeller name, synonymous all over the world with the American dollar, Nelson so far is the only conspicuous political overachiever. He has even fancied himself as a White House tenant.

Twenty years ago, a handful of liberal Republicans met in a New York City apartment to discuss the future of the Grand Old Party and the changing times. Even then the influences of the young voter, the Black, and the urban white were beginning to make the professionals realize that by the seventies the rule book for party politics would have to be rewritten. The only chance for their party was to gradually reshape its image and convince the nation it was no longer the stuffy, conservative private club of fourth-generation Americans and the super-rich.

In 1952, Nelson Rockefeller was appointed by President Eisenhower to serve as Chairman of his Advisory Committee on Government Reorganization. Besides chairing the over-all Commission, he was to focus on the specific problems at the Department of Defense. Each year the multibillion-dollar budget of the Defense Department had been criticized by members of Congress from both political parties, and the American public was sick and tired of all the waste.

Party leaders got Ike to appoint Rocky. They realized that Vice President Nixon had barely survived rough political storms during the previous election and that they had better keep at least one other Republican in the limelight so as to have a strong nominee when Ike was finished. Even then Nixon recognized Rockefeller as formidable competition and did what he could to keep his future rival for the nomination at a distance. Rockefeller had plenty of time and wasn't worried about the expenses for doing a good job. He spent more of his own money than the government did on the entire study. After a couple of years of sifting through the problems of reorganizing the Pentagon and trying to find ways to save the taxpayers' money, but still get the job done, Rockefeller returned to private life.

He was convinced that the military needed further reorganization, so he arranged to have the Rockefeller Brothers Fund, which is a small spin-off of the Rockefeller Foundation with about $90 million a year to spend on special projects of interest to the Rockefellers, jump into this study field. He put together a top group of military and civilian professionals to study what could be done to help trim defense spending. The report was prepared in 1958. As a result of a very controversial group of suggestions, Rockefeller was invited to testify before a United States Senate Committee on Armed Services, holding hearings on military preparedness. The Chairman was a future President: Lyndon Johnson.

Shortly after the Rockefeller report and Nelson's testimony in Congress, President Eisenhower announced his intention to reorganize the Defense Department. Despite complaints by Vice President Nixon, there was going to be a "price ceiling" on America's security.

Rocky first met Dr. Kissinger at the Quantico Study seminars in 1955. There a large number of experts from private foundations, educational institutions, and government agencies were meeting to discuss international problems in preparation for a series of reports to be used in briefing the President for his imminent summit conference. It was agreed by most of those at Quantico that the United States was to make a dramatic peace gesture, including a plan to prevent expansion of atomic weapons and greater international exchange of technological information.

Rockefeller got into an argument with Secretary of State John Foster Dulles as to how severe the plan would be. It was Rocky's contention that Russia was convincing most of the world's neutral nations of its peaceful intentions, and the United States was losing the philosophical war. Dulles, on the other hand, wanted to take a harder line with the Russians. Kissinger was in the middle with another group of intellectuals and scientists, who felt we had to work with the Russians to keep international power in balance, but shouldn't sacrifice too much too quickly.

The most important thing to come out of the Quantico meetings was not the dispute between Rockefeller and Dulles, or even the recommendations to President Eisenhower himself. It was the opportunity for Kissinger to go to work for the

Rockefeller Foundation and take over as a Special Studies Director. Rockefeller recognized Kissinger's talents and, thinking long-range politically, he concluded that he was a good man to have on his side.

Rockefeller is a most persuasive potential employer. "The way Nelson puts things to you—you have a public duty to accept whatever he offers, and it makes it impossible to refuse him," Kissinger later remarked to a friend after he had accepted the job.

Kissinger was immediately put into contact with such diverse political animals as General Lucius Clay, Jacob Potofsky of the Amalgamated Clothing Workers Union, and nuclear physicist Edward Teller. Rockefeller would pop in and out of the study sessions and sort of lead the way toward consensus on an approach to a particular world problem. He cajoled and prodded all the members into giving up their personal prejudices in favor of finding something in the way of a common solution. Rockefeller was a good Chairman and Kissinger was a good right-hand man.

Years later, when Kissinger was asked about Rockefeller, he gave out a statement that made Rocky's top political aides think they had a traitor in their camp.

The reporter had asked, "What kind of mind does Rockefeller have?"

Kissinger replied, "He has a second-rate mind, but a first-rate intuition about people."

The intrigued *New York Times* reporter went on to ask, "What kind of mind do you have?"

"I have a first-rate mind," Kissinger stated, without any trace of modesty, "but a third-rate intuition about people."

By the spring of 1968, it was apparent that Governor Rockefeller would be the only real opposition to Richard Nixon at the forthcoming Republican Convention in Miami.

Governor Ronald Reagan out in California was making noises like a national candidate, and could be expected to gather up a few delegate votes from the ultraconservative South. But when it came to the national scene, nobody seemed to have the money or the organization to give Nixon a run for his money except Rockefeller.

Miami Beach was to be the scene of the convention, and the Nixon forces got in early to make sure that they had total control of everything from limousines to speaker logistics at the airport when Nixon arrived. When the Rockefeller forces realized what was happening, they quickly moved in on the liberal Republicans in Florida and gathered up most of the local Democratic officials who were taken with Rocky's charisma (since most of them had relatives in New York anyway). The forgotten soul was Barry Goldwater.

Dean Burch, who later became Chairman of the Federal Communications Commission under President Nixon, was the advance man for Goldwater, along with Press Secretary Hogan Smith. Until the Goldwater aides got some help from local Democrats in Miami, they couldn't get the time of day. Somehow or other, there was no plane available to bring Goldwater to Miami International Airport from Phoenix. When he finally got there, he found that the hotel reservations had gotten loused up, and there weren't even enough tickets to the Convention floor for his guests.

I had been asked some time before to arrange transportation for Senator Goldwater through a mutual friend, General Albert F. (Dick) Lassiter, President of Executive Jet Aviation. At that time Executive Jet was rolling in dough, making millions of dollars with a rent-a-jet service for business executives and politicians. Nobody knew then that, within a couple of years, a Philadelphia District Attorney would expose Executive Jet as an illegal spin-off for moneys supposedly taken from the Pennsylvania Central Railroad, resulting in indictments of General Lassiter and others.

At the time Lassiter had provided his jet for a quick trip for Goldwater to speak in Florida at a private military school graduation where Lassiter's young son was a cadet. Now a bigger jet was needed for Goldwater. Lassiter went to work contacting his high-ranking friends in industry who realized that Goldwater was still around and that, even though Nixon couldn't publicly help him, a favor for Goldwater was a favor for Nixon. One of the largest manufacturers of cereal came on the scene with a jet large enough to accommodate Goldwater, his family, and his friends, and the entourage arrived at Miami International Airport to a hastily prepared "spontaneous reception" the day after the Convention began.

It is ironic that, when Rockefeller announced his candidacy for the Republican nomination, he gave a speech knocking Nixon's "lack of understanding of the public's criticism of the Vietnam War." Buried in the press reports of Rockefeller's announcement on May 3, 1968, when he talked about the Vietnam War and domestic problems, was a suggestion that the President of the United States should visit Red China. This idea had come from one of his new foreign affairs advisers, whom he had garnered from the staff of the Rockefeller Foundation. None other than Henry Kissinger.

It would take two and a half years for the memory of the Rockefeller suggestion for a China visit to be forgotten so as to enable Kissinger to resurrect it and make it appear as a great breakthrough for the Nixon Administration. But, for what it's worth, it was Kissinger's idea for Rocky then and his idea for Nixon later.

On August 4, 1968, the Republican Platform Committee was wrestling with the issue of Vietnam, and Rocky and Nixon found themselves in bed together. They formed a coalition to oppose the ultraconservative approach to Vietnam being argued by Governor Ronald Reagan, who wanted a strictly military solution. Senator Jacob Javits, the "liberal" from New York, met with Nixon's key aides to urge them to support a negotiated settlement idea and a quick phase-out of combat troops. Javits also suggested that everybody be included in the negotiations.

Through all the ballots at the GOP sessions, Nixon and Rockefeller arrived at the meeting and worked out a deal. Rockefeller's pride and money wouldn't permit him to step down too quickly.

On August 5th, Rockefeller came out in favor of the platform of the Republican Party as "forward-looking, progressive, and workable." It was reported that Nixon wanted Rockefeller at that time, or Senator Charles Percy of Illinois, for second place on the ticket.

Yet, Rockefeller went on "Meet the Press" and told a nationwide audience he thought Nixon wanted Reagan. This would have broken all of the traditional rules of party nominations. Even though Nixon had become a second-class New York citizen by relocating there only after becoming a very successful Wall Street lawyer, he was still thought of as a Californian. To put two from one state on the ticket was unheard of in national politics. To put two on the ticket who shared a basic conservative philosophy on so many issues was just as unheard of in these times of growing middle-of-the-road support for people like Governor Rockefeller and Senator Percy.

Rockefeller kidded Nixon by suggesting that he (Nixon) should take the Vice Presidential nomination, since he had more experience than Rockefeller.

After the Convention, it was revealed that Kissinger and a few other Rockefeller aides had outlined the somewhat dovish platform for Vietnam.

81

On August 8th, Rocky's political forces collapsed, and it became evident that, while Kissinger and the other aides who were running around seeing delegates were fine intellectual specimens, they didn't know lesson one about practical politics. At one point, an optimistic Kissinger actually told friends from Harvard that he felt they had stopped Nixon and that Rockefeller would get the nomination.

There is a good deal of conflict about just how strong the statements were that were made by Kissinger against Nixon at that time. Kissinger has repeatedly denied the vehemence that some reporters have attributed to him, when he spoke in terms of Nixon as being at best "average in politics and below average in thinking." But there seems to be no question that Kissinger did speak against Nixon to delegates from at least a dozen states and tried to argue that his election to the Presidency would mean the end of the Republican Party. On August 8th, Nelson Rockefeller was defeated, and Richard Nixon got the nomination of the Republican Party for President of the United States on the first ballot.

He was elected.

It was one of the most dramatic and tragic years in American history. The election of 1968 had seen Senator Eugene McCarthy challenge Lyndon Johnson's renomination because of his Administration's policy in the Vietnam War. Months before the Convention, Johnson suddenly announced he would not seek reelection, creating chaos in the Democratic Party and a scramble for his job. By June, the leading contender for the Democratic nomination was Senator Robert F. Kennedy, who had entered the race March 16th, only to be assassinated in June after winning the California primary. Reagan and Rockefeller had unsuccessfully challenged Nixon, who had taken the nomination to become President.

Two weeks after the Republican Convention in Miami, all

hell broke loose in Chicago. The Democrats chose Hubert H. Humphrey of Minnesota over McCarthy on the first ballot. Edmund S. Muskie of Maine was the Vice-Presidential nominee. The Democratic Party was split wide open. The nation was more concerned with the police that were injured and the hippies that were arrested, and the excuses by Mayor Richard Daley of Chicago, than they were in the platform of the Democratic Party.

Maverick George Wallace of Alabama was running as Presidential candidate of the American Independent Party and half a dozen other designations. He picked General Curtis LeMay, a reactionary relic, as his running mate, and went around the country appealing to the prejudices of anyone who would listen.

At that time few believed Wallace could garner ten million votes for the Presidency in 1968. Certainly no one realized that he would become a formidable force in the Presidential election of 1972 and sweep primaries in states right from under leading contenders of both parties.

When Nixon was nominated, he stumped the country and promised an honorable conclusion of the Vietnam War. He tried to satisfy the conservatives who had supported him by attacking "aggressors" but appeased the liberals by saying he would get out quickly.

The big issue domestically was the restoration of law and order in a country whose citizens were afraid to go onto their own streets after sundown. Humphrey was saddled with the onus of the Johnson Administration which had kept the country in the war and forced Lyndon to step aside. Wallace hoped to force the election into the House of Representatives, where his electors would hold the balance of power through their southern-state representatives. He could become a major political force.

Nixon received the lowest percentage of the popular vote of any successful candidate since Woodrow Wilson's election in 1912. One North Carolina elector threw tradition out the window and, even though he was selected to vote for Nixon, cast his vote for Wallace.

The records show that Nixon got 43.4 percent of the popular vote, while Humphrey got 42.7. Both candidates were over 31 million votes and under 32 million. Americans had to take a good hard look at their political system.

There was no way of knowing how many millions of private dollars a man like Rockefeller really spent trying to get that nomination. A top aide like Henry Kissinger doesn't come cheaply. According to one estimate, the campaigns of that year had cost a record $300 million, which meant an increase of over 52 percent in only four years. The Republicans won, but had to out-spend the Democrats almost two to one. Most of the jump in cost was reflected in the enormous expenses for television. Of course, the candidacy of two multi-millionaires, Governor Nelson Rockefeller and the late Senator Robert Kennedy, didn't help matters.

One study made on that election was Herb Alexander's "Financing the 1968 Election," which was itself financed by the Citizens Research Foundation of Princeton.

He reported that Senator Eugene McCarthy of Minnesota, who everyone thought was running a poor man's campaign, spent $11 million. Senator Robert Kennedy spent $9 million (the same amount that third-party candidate George Wallace of Alabama did). This financing was amassed from the greatest collection of small funds in the history of this country. Rockefeller, who never got that nomination and didn't really get off the ground in the primaries, reported that he had unloaded $8 million.

When the votes were counted, Nixon was the first President since Zachary Taylor in 1848 not to have his own party win at least one chamber of Congress in his initial election to the White House. The big mystery, however, was where that 13 percent of Americans who voted for George Wallace had come from. Although the largest number of voters, in excess of 73 million, turned out at the polls, it was only 60 percent of those who could have voted.

Nixon wasted no time in putting his team together. He immediately met with Governor Rockefeller and offered him the position of United Nations Ambassador. He also suggested David Rockefeller as Secretary of the Treasury, a position justified by the latter's banking experience. Nelson wasn't interested, though he might have taken Secretaryship of State or Defense. Nixon didn't offer them.

It was then that Nixon sent for Kissinger and had his secret meeting at the Hotel Pierre in New York, after which Kissinger was awarded the title of Assistant to the President for National Security Affairs. He had come a long way since his naturalization in 1943. Much of it he owed to Rockefeller, and Kissinger discussed his offer from Nixon with Rocky in three separate meetings. Rockefeller was not displeased. It not only meant that he would have a good contact inside the White House, but that perhaps some of his own ideas would filter into foreign affairs.

The rest of the Nixon team was going to be coordinated by controversial Robert H. Finch, Nixon's buddy from California. He carried the title of Counselor to the President, along with Donald Rumsfeld. Kissinger's domestic counterpart was another German, John D. Ehrlichman, who was helped by Peter M. Flanigan and H. R. Haldeman.

The former Army private, who had been a brush salesman,

who had served as interpreter for a General, and who had taken over a district in Germany, was now given his own private Brigadier General as an aide.

In the excitement of the first few months of organizing the White House staff, most people forgot that Kissinger had been so vocal in Miami Beach against Nixon's becoming President.

And by June 1, 1969, Patrick Anderson could quote in the *New York Times Magazine* a philosophic quip by Kissinger: "Seen one President, you've seen them all."

CHAPTER 8

———— ✠ ————

INTRODUCING THE NIXINGERS

Henry Kissinger met Richard Nixon for the first time when both men dined at the home of Clare Boothe Luce in 1967. Henry had heard his colleagues putting Nixon down for years as an intellectual misfit and political hand-me-down.

Neither the Ambassador-publisher nor Nixon anticipated that it would be the Luce *Time-Life* empire that would catapult Kissinger into a continuous world spotlight.

Mrs. Luce is a grand dame who splits her time between her Hawaiian castle and her New York publishing throne. She enjoys mixing politicians, writers, and traveling academicians —even if they are Jews. She introduced Nixon to Kissinger. The man who would become President was quick to compliment Henry on his writings. He was genuinely impressed to meet such a thinker.

Kissinger was not won over. A year or so later he and most Republican thinkers were trying to stop Nixon from getting the nomination. It was the GOP Convention. Miami was getting hot with possible race riots across the bay from the Fontainebleau Hotel.

The Convention was getting hot too. Senator Barry Goldwater would arrive that afternoon to try to stop the South from going for California Governor Ronald Reagan. Nixon needed those votes. Meanwhile Kissinger and the Rockefeller forces were fighting for delegates' promises to stop Nixon from winning a first-ballot victory.

It was an unfortunate time for Kissinger to be asked for an evaluation of his future boss, but a wire service reporter asked Henry what he thought of Nixon as a man. The pressure had been great for several days, and Kissinger wasn't sleeping nights. The word slipped out and the future adviser to the President was stuck with it. "Ridiculous," Kissinger said. The reporter pressed him and asked for his opinion of Nixon as President. "Even more ridiculous," Kissinger added.

Even though Henry had felt Nixon to be a loser, the Whittier flash was taken with the kinky Professor. Kissinger typified those insulated thinkers who run from country to country on the highest academic tracks and drop in and out of governments at will, giving out with a white paper here and a lecture there.

A mark of achievement for Kissinger's pen had been *Nuclear Weapons and Foreign Policy*, which was published in 1957. Among the more significant letters of congratulations from colleagues and admirers was a short note from Richard Nixon, Vice President of the United States. Just prior to the 1959 summit meeting, Kissinger had written in the *New York Times* a warning against trusting the Russians. This dovetailed beautifully with Nixon's own tough philosophy.

Neither man could then foresee that Kissinger would become the softening agent for President Nixon's rapprochements with both the Russians and the Chinese in 1972.

Nearly ten years after that summit meeting, when Nixon was stumping for the Presidency, Kissinger was invited to join his Foreign Policy Advisory Committee and help draft position papers. He declined. Then Nixon won the election. After having turned down one opportunity in a campaign and never having been quoted as saying anything favorable about the man, Kissinger was astonished to get a call from Dwight L. Chapin, Nixon's personal aide. Chapin told Henry that Nixon wanted to meet with him quietly at the Pierre Hotel in New York, which has been the scene of high-level party conferences (and a sensational robbery or two).

As Kissinger donned his traditional conservative suit and New England striped tie, he considered all the possibilities. He concluded that Nixon wanted his opinion on those who had been invited to join the new State Department and other government agencies dealing with foreign policy. The man who was soon to be called "Herr Super-Kraut" was easily able to put aside any second thoughts as to why Nixon would ask someone for advice who had been a political enemy. He remembered his stature in the community of thinkers, and his vanity did the rest.

Kissinger was right. Nixon opened that quiet meeting at the Pierre with a Scotch and soda and talked about some of his proposed nominees for key foreign service slots. Halfway through the conversation, Kissinger began to realize that he was among those whom Nixon expected to serve on his team. In his own half-blunt, half-obscure way, the President-elect of the United States was offering this German-Jewish stranger the most important job in foreign policy, Director of the National Security Council.

The irony was that here was a respected man who, in no conditions, would have joined forces with Candidate Nixon. But now he was being asked to join the forces of President-elect Nixon. After he got over the shock and the surprise, he was impressed that Nixon had called on him. During the week that followed, Henry consulted with Governor Rockefeller and other anti-Nixon friends. They were reassured to think that the President-elect would select Henry for such a position. Arthur Schlesinger, Jr., Kissinger's mentor, had been a White House regular for years, and he led the choir of intellectual praise for Henry's appointment.

Eight days after the offer, the die was cast. Kissinger accepted. A man who barely knew the President was to be his chief foreign policy adviser. A man who had been associated with the liberal Republican enemies of Richard Nixon would be his right-hand man. They would try to end a war, make some friends, and remedy America's shrinking stature.

Other Presidents had developed foreign affairs protégés as they worked their way up the political ladder. But Nixon had no protégés and very few friends.

It took less than a month for Kissinger to become not only the most powerful figure on foreign policy in this country, but the second most powerful man in the United States government.

Most of the reports concerning the appointment of William D. Rogers as Secretary of State were inaccurate. One was excellent. Reporters Rowland Evans, Jr., and Robert D. Novak in their syndicated column realized that Kissinger's success as Nixon's Prime Minister could not have been achieved had it not been for the uniqueness of the appointment of William P. Rogers. The Secretary of State-to-be had one thing in common with Kissinger: He didn't help Nixon get elected President. He had said repeatedly he would play no part in the Nixon Administration. Despite their past friendship which dated back to Nixon's Communist-hunting congressional days in the late forties, Bill Rogers took no part in the campaign.

There were reasons.

After serving as a lawyer for the Senate investigating committee, Rogers had traveled with Nixon on the Vice Presidential campaign plane. He was an all-purpose political aide, late-evening drinking partner, and shoulder to cry on. After Rogers became Deputy Attorney General in the Eisenhower Administration, he renewed his close friendship with Nixon during those precarious months after the President's heart attack when no one knew whether Eisenhower's heart would last.

By 1968, the Nixon-Rogers friendship had become reduced to meetings at occasional social gatherings and an exchange of gifts at holiday time. Rogers was getting very rich as a lawyer in New York and Washington, D.C. He was taking every advantage of his connections in government. His principal client was Mrs. Phillip R. Graham, publisher of *Newsweek* Magazine and the *Washington Post*. Rogers kept telling his Wall Street buddies he couldn't afford the luxury of going back into politics. "I enjoy being rich," he said.

Nixon was looking around, now that he had become President-elect, for a Secretary of State who could effectively represent the Nixon philosophy. At the same time his man needed an individual image for the American people. His first choice was Governor William Scranton of Pennsylvania, who had had more ups and downs than any political yo-yo since Harold Stassen. The President-elect, who has probably set a record for being turned down by would-be appointees, quickly found out that Scranton would not accept the job.

The prestigious Council of Foreign Relations suggested C. Douglas Dillon, who was top man in the Wall Street house of Dillon Read. As a big GOP contributor, Dillon had bought his way into the Eisenhower Administration as Under Secretary of State and gotten to know Nixon well.

Richard Nixon plays the game of politics seriously, and Dillon never had a chance. He had neglected to go through the motions of asking Nixon's approval before becoming a token Republican as President John F. Kennedy's Secretary of the Treasury in 1961. Besides, Nixon suffered from a justified social inferiority complex. He and Pat had been snubbed by the old-line Republican families of New York when Nixon gave up the vineyards of California for the retainers of Wall Street. He blamed Dillon for not having come to his help in breaking into a few of the right clubs, right restaurants, and right society events.

After considering Scranton and Dillon as banner-carriers in foreign policy, Nixon turned to the crusty old former Governor of New York, Thomas E. Dewey, for help. Dewey pushed for Rogers. This was ridiculous. Rogers had no experience in foreign policy except having gone through gestures as a function attender for the Mission Team of the United Nations. Besides, Rogers wasn't particularly interested in foreign affairs. On the other hand, what could be better qualifications for a Secretary of State destined to play second banana to Henry Kissinger?

The selection of Rogers as Secretary of State enabled Kissinger to become the powerhouse in Washington. When Nixon offered the job to Bill Scranton, he knew that his nominee was a scrappy independent. He would have been a heavy at the State Department, and probably would have dominated the Cabinet. He obviously wasn't picked because he got along with Nixon or was even necessarily loyal to the Nixon ideas on how to treat the world. But he had the personal ability, and Nixon felt that, if he was going to play politics with the rest of the Cabinet, one good solid appointment could mean support in the country.

Why, then, would the President of the United States settle for a man whose only real value as Secretary of State would be that he'd keep quiet, nod, and be loyal? Probably it was because Nixon was ill equipped to put together a proper Cabinet and staff. He realized that carefully studied appointments would probably result in effectively filling only one-tenth of the top jobs. Haste literally made waste, and the names were filled in without much thought.

Machiavelli said, "The first impression one gets of a ruler and of his brains is from seeing the men that he has about him." Constantly preoccupied with what people were thinking about him, Nixon certainly realized that his appointment of Kissinger would at least reflect credit on his ability to pick people. "Even if they don't think Nixon is an intellect, they must realize that he at least has enough brains to recognize an intellect," one of the White House staff said lightly, after the selection of Kissinger. It was a poignant comment.

Kissinger was the most unlikely member of "the German trio," as three top Nixon aides came to be known. The second member is H. R. (Bob) Haldeman, whose official title is simply Assistant to the President. He got his training for White House service at the J. Walter Thompson Advertising Agency after getting a Bachelor's degree in business management from UCLA. His chief qualification for service in the White House was having done public relations advance work for Richard Nixon in 1956 and 1960. He also managed the disastrous Nixon campaign for Governor of California that had everyone thinking Nixon was politically dead.

Is experience as a campaign technician sufficient to qualify as administrator of billions of taxpayers' money? Haldeman's talent in handling vital domestic programs remains to be found. Haldeman shares one basic Nixon emotion, and that is hostility toward the press. The President can be sure that Haldeman will never leak anything. He can also be sure he will get regular reports of insults by his second German guard to members of the Washington press corps.

Haldeman is also known as the poet laureate of blunt, in-

93

sulting, quick poetry in the White House. His memos would make a best-seller of high pressure and crude outlines of this nation's problems.

Haldeman was thrust upon the national scene with his title-waving and the support of the President much in the same manner as Kissinger. But there was no competition between the two, since Haldeman's educational and intellectual assets can't hold a candle to Henry's. His first tie with the President came when Nixon was leading the anti-Communist investigations for the House Committee on Un-American activities in the late 1940's. Haldeman was one of the few students at UCLA who supported the Red-hunters.

Haldeman is a total conservative. He started out with a basic suspicion toward all members of the press, Blacks, students, radical leaders, labor leaders, anyone critical of Nixon, and other members of the White House staff. This was enough to keep him very busy and closeted with his own philosophical hang-ups.

After Nixon took office, Haldeman was paired with another German, John D. Ehrlichman, who became Assistant to the President for Domestic Affairs. They took personal philosophy and made it policy in the government of the United States.

Ehrlichman's tie with Nixon also dated back to college days. He and Haldeman were classmates at UCLA and even fellow Eagle Scouts. They attended the Christian Scientist Church together and joined in abstaining from liquor and tobacco, although some of their other vices seem to have shown staying power. In 1960, Haldeman had brought his buddy Ehrlichman into the Nixon campaign. He involved him again two years later for the losing California Governor's race. In 1966, Ehrlichman sat it out. He was a late arrival for the 1968 Presidential campaign, showing up at the Miami Beach Convention after the decision had already been made. Ehrlichman was supposed to coordinate the campaign and pull all details together for every campaign stop. He covered everything from the number of pretty girls wearing Nixon banners, to where each Mayor should stand. He was also supposed to keep track of who had to get "thank you" letters for the bigger contributions and who was promised post offices and new jobs.

When Ehrlichman arrived at the White House for his reward in 1969, he was given a routine assignment. Haldeman pushed his buddy, and Ehrlichman rapidly rose to the political surface and grabbed some authority from others less well connected with Nixon.

Haldeman's office was known as the Berlin Wall, guarding the President. The public relations man made it impossible for top government advisers to get to Nixon on vital topics. There is no question that this policy of protective custody resulted in resignation after resignation by key people. It produced some vacuums.

When a vacuum was created in a top domestic policy slot in the White House, Ehrlichman was shoved in by Haldeman and welcomed by Nixon.

To the rest of the Republican hierarchy, and to the press and democratic critics, Haldeman and Ehrlichman looked as close as Tweedle-Dee and Tweedle-Dum. There were a few differences. Haldeman's mind was closed and he admitted it. Ehrlichman's mind was closed, but he denied it. He went through the motions of meeting outsiders and was almost cordial to the press.

Balancing Haldeman and Ehrlichman was easy by staying just a bit to the left of the President on every issue. A German superstructure in the White House created problems Nixon didn't sense.

The arrogance and totalitarian attitude of his key employees turned off middle-of-the-road reporters. They hadn't made up their minds about Nixon. But Nixon's aides fixed that—the wrong way.

Kissinger became the third and vital link in the Teutonic chain. He climaxed the image of Nixon's insulation from the country and his insistence that all power be under his control.

Nixon's first meeting with Kissinger ended with a specific order. The President reportedly asked the man who would become Professor - turned - Adviser - turned - Secret - Agent: "Henry, tell me where the United States stands today in Europe, Southeast Asia, and the Middle East. . . . How can I set up a National Security Council in the White House to function? . . . What are my crises, and what will they be? . . . What should I do concerning the strategic arms limitation (SALT) talks?"

The very specific nature of Nixon's assignment keynoted the Kissinger operation. Despite the sarcasm of his critics, there is no way to dilute the efforts of Henry Kissinger in answering those questions. He gives the President enough options to keep the country alive.

During those early days in the White House, even Henry was forced to curtail his social life. Late-night snacks in the Situation Room replaced late-night situations in his bedroom. Nixon had a bad war on his hands and Kissinger had to try to get him out. There would be little chance to pull the country together (or get reelected) if something wasn't done. The Kissinger approach to the military problem was based on his standard come-on to a good-looking woman. Analyze, impress with your authority, bluff a little, work like hell, insist on winning, score, and move on!

Kissinger was able to bury himself in his power and his work. The secret agent in every little boy who envisions himself leading a Mission Impossible took over. As a little boy, he

96

hadn't had the chance to play much. Now, he would make the most of it. Haldeman and Ehrlichman were relegated to second string on the Nixon team. The President was hypnotized by Kissinger's logical mind and liked the way Henry made him look good.

Life at the White House with Richard Nixon was staid in many ways. Nixon hated the casual barbecue method that LBJ used in dealing with his aides. He was formal and proper—almost ritualistic. The President is one of those who might just as well not wear a sport shirt. It doesn't show. He looks no different.

White House luncheons for the National Security Council were dropped. Under Kissinger, there were work groups.

Kissinger's ascent to power had begun even before the President took office. On the eve of his inauguration, Nixon summoned Kissinger to Key Biscayne. (The little restricted island off the coast of Miami also housed Bebe Rebozo, Nixon's partner in golf, fishing, fun, and property.) He wanted his proposal for reorganizing the National Security Council.

When Henry arrived, the President-elect was getting ready to tee off for a last nine holes before returning to Washington. Kissinger's lengthy memorandum would require several hours' study to assimilate it properly. The memo might just as well have said that Cleveland, Ohio, was to be sold to Bolivia. Nixon looked at the first page, smiled, asked for a pen, and signed. And that was how the National Security Council was reorganized. It was a significant demonstration of the degree of confidence Richard Nixon had in Henry Kissinger even at that early point.

It didn't take Kissinger and Nixon long to know that their marriage would work out. The President was limited to well-turned phrases designed to grab votes; Kissinger could turn out erudite position papers. At heart, Nixon felt the world needed to return to an old-fashioned balance of power; Kissinger agreed, and would tolerate Nixon at the helm to get it.

The first meeting of the new National Security Council in the White House was the turning point in recent foreign policy in this country. Kissinger took over. The combination of his pragmatic, forceful presentation with the script he and his staff had drafted gave him complete command. After that the meetings became monologues.

Vietnam, of course, was the continuing critical problem that threatened Nixon's future political success. At first Kissinger gave the President options on everything, enabling Nixon to select one of the solutions Henry suggested. In the early days of the new Administration, the combat-oriented Generals and Admirals at the Pentagon would no doubt have been a lot happier with Kissinger running the military than Secretary of Defense Melvin Laird. Laird had softened and was talking in terms of peace—almost as if it was desirable. But Kissinger had come to the White House convinced that the South Vietnamese would never become a fighting force that could win anything against Hanoi or even defeat the Vietcong guerrillas in the south. In his view there was plenty of work in Southeast Asia for U.S. Generals and Admirals.

As Kissinger's stature increased, the Defense Department reached a sort of detente with the man who was Special Assistant to the President for Foreign Affairs and head of the National Security Council. Kissinger has carefully avoided getting involved in the mechanics of the Pentagon operation and has left to the military the tactical decisions necessary to beef up policy decisions. He prefers to work on the higher level of making plans and letting lesser officials like the Secretary of Defense carry them out. The Generals keep their internal power and image, and Kissinger continues to acquire power.

On September 29, 1971, White House Press Secretary

Ronald Ziegler, in a slip of the tongue, unconsciously promoted Henry by introducing him as Secretary of State Kissinger. The embarrassed young press aide quickly corrected himself and declared the slip off the record. The irony of that phrase was that all of official Washington recognized that Kissinger was indeed Secretary of State with some extra special powers thrown in.

The Kissinger role in the Nixon Administration has caused the bluntest exile of a Secretary of State since Abraham Lincoln dumped Jeremiah S. Black for William H. Seward. But there have been other instances when the Secretary of State was more figurehead than fact. When Franklin Delano Roosevelt appointed Cordell Hull as his Secretary of State, many laughed. While Hull knew Latin America, they knew it was FDR's White House buddy, Harry Hopkins, who would really advise the President on foreign affairs. During John F. Kennedy's Administration, critics said we had no need for a Secretary of State. Dean Rusk went through the motions, but Kennedy was his own foreign minister.

The Secretary of State is head of a giant government department that relies on Congress for budget approval. He is at the legislators' mercy and must respond to their questions, even though his testimony may be an "empty exercise." A White House aide is above all that.

Kissinger has consistently hidden behind "executive privilege" when the Senate Foreign Relations Committee called. It is not an enviable task to face the pointed questions of Committee Chairman J. William Fulbright, as Dean Rusk can attest. The antiquated idea of executive privilege is based on the theory that there is a confidential relationship between the President and his top aides. It allows the White House to send Kissinger only when it is politically advantageous.

Kissinger's role as de facto Secretary of State has not gone without opposition. Senator Stuart Symington is a no-nonsense guy who may have forgotten more about the Armed Services than most men in government now know. The tall Missouri Democrat had been Secretary of the Air Force in the Truman Administration, United States Senator since 1953, and a leading Democratic Presidential contender back in 1960 when John Kennedy won the nomination and election.

With that background, Symington did not hesitate to speak out, and he shook up Washington when he challenged the Nixon-Kissinger-Rogers relationship. The Senator really intended to knock off two birds with one speech. First, he believed the Senate had a right to know what was going on in the White House war rooms. The bills for Vietnam were astronomical. There were shifts of American troops all over the globe. American policy in the Middle East was hazy, to say the least.

Secondly, he wanted to help an old friend, Bill Rogers. (You remember him—the Secretary of State.) Kissinger had become a Rasputin with fantastic influence on U.S. foreign policy and unprecedented authority in American diplomacy. Symington didn't mince words. "Wherever one goes around this town," he said, "one hears our very able Secretary of State laughed at. People say he's Secretary of State in title only."

The President was upset. The harsh attack by a respected U.S. Senator confirmed what most of Washington and the press corps already knew. Nixon, a full-time politician, spends many hours each week measuring the points he has won or lost. With Symington's blast, he had lost quite a few. The State Department formally denied the charges of the Senator from Missouri. Informally, half a dozen key Congressmen and Senators close to the Nixingers had to have reassurances. "Rogers is my oldest and closest friend in the Cabinet. . . .

He is the foreign policy adviser for the President. . . . He is the chief foreign policy spokesman for the President."

Nixon was unconvincing. The Senator's charges stuck. Still the episode didn't do much for William Rogers. In months to come, the White House would reveal twelve secret meetings between the unofficial Secretary of State Henry Kissinger and North Vietnamese officials in Paris.

Nixon's projected visit to China would become a reality in late February of 1972, capped with Kissinger's announcing the results of the historic sessions.

After China, there would be secret meetings with the Russians, and finally a summit session in Moscow in May, 1972.

By 1972, Kissinger's ascension to power had become so obvious that, when newsmen were briefed on the background for a Presidential decision, it was Kissinger who did it. When foreign diplomats screamed, they wanted Kissinger. Meanwhile there were rumblings from the State Department that the White House was undermining its role in government. As a result, a few token meetings were being set up through Foggy Bottom, the more-than-ever appropriate nickname for the Department of State. It describes Secretary Rogers' influence—foggy and at the bottom.

The eclipse of the Secretary of State was more total than that of any of his predecessors, and Kissinger's ascendancy to awesome power was also without precedent. The two men offer a revealing contrast in personality and background. Rogers is the small-town boy who became an Establishment lawyer by constant compromise, and leads a conservative life. Kissinger is the forceful immigrant from Nazi Germany who appears to be the articulate master of any international problem, and enough of a swinger to delight the press. He is also the only colorful character in the blandest Administration

101

since Eisenhower's. Rogers, by contrast, is a sincere, low-key, quiet man, with no big stick apparent.

The big factor in Kissinger's takeover of foreign policy has been his regular down-the-hall access to the President. Former aides swear Nixon sees more of Henry than Pat. It is the daily quick briefings on everything from Hanoi to heroin that keep Kissinger on top. He gives his boss a chance to relax.

The Nixinger government is a peculiar blending of two men who look at world problems in similar fashion, despite their far-apart origins. Nixon built his reputation as a hard-liner. He has never been noted for his appeal to minorities or intellectuals. Suddenly, there appears on the scene a Jewish Professor nurtured in the liberal Republican camp of Nelson Rockefeller. He might easily have been a questionable candidate for the top foreign policy slot because of his religion. Certainly he would seem to have been disqualified by his anti-Nixon efforts at the Republican Convention that nominated the President. Even his Harvard roots could be suspect to an academically deficient Administration. Yet, in less than four years he became the most powerful adviser in the world—and probably the all-time apostle for academicians.

Rogers' willingness to play second fiddle to Kissinger has manifestly hurt the State Department. Its prestige is sagging. "Kissinger has been too visible," a top Rogers aide has admitted. "The Secretary must assert himself and stop being retiring."

It's too late. Not even Madison Avenue's image makers could foist Rogers on the American public as more than a political puppet.

The other influential men on Nixon's team have accepted Henry's conquest. John Mitchell, the dry Campaign Manager who used his Attorney Generalship to try to keep American consensus with Nixon, likes Kissinger. But he does not view him as a competitor.

He considers that, like every other technician, Henry is expendable. If a major Kissinger global proposal should go sour, Henry could be out! Mitchell, on the other hand, can soundly reason that, as long as Nixon is in politics, his own expertise in getting the money and votes to win an election will be essential—even though he no longer officially is Campaign Manager.

But there are some problems. Enamored by Kissinger's foreign affairs strength, Nixon had begun to rely on Henry for decisions involving domestic matters as the 1972 Presidential election drew near. Despite his intellect, Kissinger is a political novice. He was totally ineffective in Rockefeller's failing campaign, while Nixon's professionals were accomplishing the selling of a President. Kissinger has never been elected to anything. He doesn't relate philosophy to individual reactions, but stays on a global force level. Nixon's reliance on the Professor for guidance on local issues scares the Republican National Committee members. Those worthies consider Kissinger's image a double-edged sword. Some respect Nixon's use of a fine scholar. Others are instinctively suspicious—seeing Henry as a Strangelovian character who might embroil the United States in a cataclysmic war. Anyway, they ask, aren't all college professors crazy?

You could hear sentiments like that at GOP headquarters throughout the country in 1972, and John Mitchell and other top campaign strategists began wondering if it wouldn't be better if Kissinger were closeted away from public view during the campaign season.

All things considered, the Nixinger Administration couldn't afford to take anything for granted in the election year of 1972.

CHAPTER 9

---　✢　---

NATIONAL SECURITY COUNCIL

"There cannot be a crisis next week. My schedule is already full."
—HENRY KISSINGER (as quoted in the *New York Times Magazine*, June 1, 1969)

Henry may be trying to become a manmade reincarnation of one of his great heroes, Klemens Metternich. In his day, that Austrian statesman epitomized the shrewd, all-powerful, international balance-of-power diplomat. Kissinger wrote his graduate thesis about Metternich's masterly control of European politics in the nineteenth century and, judging from Henry's present role, he learned his lessons well. As Nixon's personal emissary to everywhere on everything, Kissinger has become *the* authoritative carrier of American policy—second only to the President.

At Harvard, Henry's colleagues surmised that he had vaulting ambitions for public life. Now that he is a public servant of unique distinction, he may have exceeded even his own expectations. Since he cannot be President (only native-born citizens can hold that office), in power terms he has gone about as far as he can go in the United States. He no longer merely presents options on national security for Nixon to evaluate and select from. Kissinger now is the molder of major policy, and influences foreign affairs as much as the President himself.

Although he is saddled with the National Security Council as a base from which to move, Kissinger's personal belief appears to be that the most efficient body politic is a constituency of one—and that one is Kissinger.

During those meetings in late 1968 when Nixon and Kissinger tried to decide exactly what Henry's role would be, several suggestions were made. Kissinger would not leave the Washington scene to accept a major Ambassadorship. First, he was too poor to support himself in the style to which Ambassadors like to become accustomed. Second, he would never be able to limit himself mentally to the problems of one nation. When Nixon invited Henry to accept the post of foreign policy assistant and suggested that a political transfusion be given the near-defunct National Security Council, Kissinger accepted.

The Council had been set up under Harry Truman after World War II, and supposedly it was a planning body designed to create long-range programs for Presidential approval. It had become obscure under Truman's successors, but Nixon thought it was a perfect instrument to bring control of foreign affairs back from the State Department to the White House. Nixon has always feared being faced with specific decisions without alternatives. The NSC as a planning group with somebody like Kissinger at the helm could provide him with enough options to satisfy him in every major field.

Kissinger became the President's options man. The power to select options presumes a good deal of power to influence decisions, since the options man simply would not present alternatives that he considered unthinkable. Henry had a lot of power right from the start.

When Nixon initialed Kissinger's blueprints for the National Security Council at Key Biscayne just before his inauguration, it meant the political demise of the Secretary of State, and the major decisions on American involvement in everything from the Vietnam War to the Middle East shifted to the basement of the White House even before the Secretary of State had settled in at Foggy Bottom.

Nixon has exploited the bonus of "executive privilege" that comes with Kissinger. As confidential adviser to the President he has successfully invoked that privilege as a way of minimizing Congressional interference, hiding behind the cloak of executive immunity when asked to testify as to where millions of dollars were being spent. This was the essence of the complaints of Senator Symington and others. Even when the Secretary of State testifies before a Congressional committee, it is a prepared statement that usually leaves more questions unanswered than answered. And when answers are forthcoming, the legislators realize that it is only second-level propaganda—that they have not gotten to the man at the heart of the decision-making process.

The policy of not allowing a top Presidential aide to testify on the record is not new. The problem is that the Nixinger Administration has penetrated more deeply than most previous Administrations into the operations of more government departments. Wherever Congress turns to try to get the facts, it is likely to be stymied—to find that all roads lead to Kissinger's Council chambers.

The activities in those chambers follow a fairly regular pattern. Hugh Sidney in *Life* (February 11, 1972) gives a vivid picture of a typical meeting. At least once a week, the members of the National Security Council gather in the Cabinet room to await the President. The Secretary of State is there, together with his Defense counterpart, Melvin Laird; and George Lincoln, the Director of the Office of Emergency

107

Preparedness. Even the Vice President shows up occasionally.

Top intelligence experts from the Central Intelligence Agency (CIA), Department of Defense, and various military units come loaded with special reports. Behind the conference tables, aides sit silently. Secretaries Rogers and Laird flank the President's empty chair. Most of the others study the agenda and try to anticipate the questions that will be forthcoming. Then the man enters—not the President of the United States —but Henry Kissinger. Traditionally he carries a black notebook in one hand which blends with his black or banker's-blue suit. He strides a bit more majestically now that he has made the covers of *Newsweek* and *Time*. But he still looks a little funny, and generally an aide has to suppress a chuckle at the high forehead and the peacocklike manner. "Good morning, Bill . . . Mel . . . Dick . . . Mr. Vice President." He moves to his place at the left of the President's chair. He brings out his notebook.

The others can judge how long the meeting will last by the thickness of Kissinger's notebook. There is only one other copy of his notes, and they are placed in front of the President under the watchful eyes of his security guard.

(One observer commented that he had often wondered about Kissinger's air of authority. Then one day it dawned on him that, while the others entered from the door on the far left of the room, Kissinger always came in from the right—the office of the President.)

Kissinger alone knows what Nixon's thoughts are on today's agenda, and he will see to it that the meeting goes exactly as the President wants. Everyone at the meeting must be aware that they are merely going through motions. Decisions were already made by Kissinger and the President earlier in the day. Henry was with the President that morning . . . the night before . . . and most of the nights and days of weeks before.

The impressive titles of those around the desk are meaningless. The protocol of who sits closest to the Chief Executive is also misleading. This is Henry's playground and his ball and his rules and, if you want to play, that is the way it must be.

"Gentlemen, the President of the United States," an aide announces. Nixon lopes through the door with a cheery "Good morning," and settles into the chair in the middle of the table. Everyone seems intimidated by the President's presence except Kissinger.

Nixon opens the meeting by announcing why he has called it and what the specific problem to be decided is. He then looks to his left and routinely says, "Henry, will you present the options for us?" Kissinger clears his throat (as he does every couple of minutes) and, for twenty-five minutes without interruption, states the options in steady, clear, accented terms. Nixon sits back and smiles while Kissinger goes on presenting the options he has reviewed earlier that day. It is obvious that the President is proud of the presentation, perhaps hoping that somebody will think he told Henry what to say instead of the opposite being true. Henry becomes the Professor for everyone present. He is back at Harvard; and his students are the Cabinet, the Vice President, and top intelligence aides. He breaks down each option clinically and even pauses to explain a difficult word or two.

Sometimes he picks up his notes and quotes himself, and other times he goes on for minutes at a time without reference assistance.

Nixon has his own notebook (also prepared by Kissinger), and it contains a summary of the issues and points for the President to make. Most of the time he follows it. Nobody in the audience has any serious challenges for a Kissinger presentation. Nobody will express his opinions on the options until he gets a tip-off in a phrase, expression, or gesture by either the President or Henry. Nobody in the Nixon Administration can afford to be on the "wrong" side of a major issue. (Remember former Secretary of the Interior Walter J. Hickel?)

Nixon will poll the table, but he asks his questions in such a way as to make it perfectly clear what answers he wants. There are a couple of suggestions as to procedure, and the discussion turns to how to get the people of the United States and Congress to accept whatever it is the Administration is going to do.

The meeting ends, and the Cabinet officers with their aides in their wake scurry out the door on their left for their limousines. Kissinger tucks his huge notebook under his arm and strides off down the hall, often to be stopped by the President saying, "Henry, can you join me for a moment?" They walk off huddled together, deciding the fate of America and possibly the world.

The relationship between Kissinger and the President is genuinely close. Once Nixon had determined to bring in the Professor from the Rockefeller camp, he never regretted it. What Kissinger lacked in political experience, he made up for in his uncanny ability to express things explicitly and in the Nixon tone. As Henry has weathered storm after storm in foreign affairs, the President and he have reached an understanding. The President articulated his feelings in January, 1971, after Henry's return from one of the secret meetings with the North Vietnamese. Nixon told a press conference that he had written to Henry and said: "Frankly, I cannot imagine what the government would be like without you. . . . I am grateful for what you have done, and I am grateful that you are staying."

There had been rumors that Kissinger would leave so as not to invoke the academic wrath of Harvard and lose his Professorship. The policy of cutting off top people who are not on campus to teach after a couple of years was inflexible. Somewhere along the way Kissinger decided to stay on at the White House and let his future take care of itself.

If you were to ask the man in the street, "Who is Brigadier General Alexander M. Haig?" he might answer, "The commanding officer of that outfit that was involved in the big bloody battle in Vietnam." Few realize that Haig carries the impressive title of Deputy Assistant to the President for National Security Affairs. That is his title, but his function is to serve as top assistant to Henry A. Kissinger. He can move the Pentagon into action for his boss quicker than the Joint Chiefs of Staff can.

The Council staff includes an impressive roster of other aides for Kissinger, including David R. Halperin, Robert G. Houdek, Commander Jonathan T. Howe, Thomas K. Latimer, Winston Lord, Peter W. Rodman, and David R. Young.

In addition to the regular staff, the NSC retains intelligence personnel for Latin America, Europe, Africa, East Asia, the Near East, South Asia, international economic affairs, scientific affairs, and United Nations matters. Colonel Richard T. Kennedy is Director of a ten-man planning group which does the preliminary drafting of the option plans that Kissinger reviews with his staff before presenting them to the President.

Kissinger's brain trust is known as the Program Analysis Staff. Their job is to make sure that the Professor does not goof when presenting a report to the Council or the President. They have to be sure that nothing is going to contravene any new bill that has come out of Congress or even violate something the President may have said in a speech a few weeks before. Another function of the Program Staff is to study what

111

leaders of foreign countries are saying so as to predict how receptive they will be to Henry's latest ideas. Wayne Smith was the Director of the group and became the fourteenth top Kissinger aide to quit when he resigned to take a high-paying job in industry in California. He told the *New York Times* that it was not really policy differences that had caused his departure, "I'm just too tired to work with Henry. The pressure is too intense, and it is not worth it."

For all the staff members, the job is rough. Henry seems to have a fiendish delight in coming in earlier and leaving later than his employees and being able to keep up a busy international social life while never falling behind in his work. The Professor is as difficult to see as the President himself. Two assistants quit specifically because they could not get to Henry with their ideas or criticisms. Now his dozen or so senior aides see him at least once a month, and their staff assistants hear about their good work through them.

"Working for Henry," one former aide told *Newsweek*, "you learn never to say to him, 'Thank you, Henry.' He doesn't like it; it embarrasses him. He does lots of little things, personal things, that you want to thank him for; but you cannot do it if you know what's good for you."

Kissinger also controls a web of interdepartmental groups and committees that operate at the level of Assistant Secretaries of State and Defense. He delegates very little to his fellow Council members, and prefers to serve as Chairman of all the important panels, groups, and committees. If for any reason he is not available, one of his staff men presides to make sure the group follows the Kissinger line.

After his first year in charge, Kissinger decided on some changes in the NSC. He eliminated the emphasis on long-term policy planning and worked more on today and tomorrow. The quickest way to get answers in government is to pay for them, so the National Security Council budget was increased from $132,000 to a half million dollars for outside consultants. Kissinger then brought in key people in every specialty for a review of agency reports.

The basic criticism in Washington of the Kissinger National Security operation is that, when requests for information are sent out, they are framed in such a way as to program the answer. The White House vehemently denies that Nixon is trying to control the policies of all government agencies through Kissinger, but the political reality of life with the Nixingers is that they do not have much confidence in anyone but themselves.

Bureaucracy gets confusing at the Council staff level. For example, Jeanne W. Davis carries the title of Staff Secretary to the National Security Council Staff Secretariat of the Office of the Assistant to the President for National Security Affairs. John Osborne wrote a penetrating article for the *New Republic* describing Kissinger as "so burdened with the President's demands and with National Security Council business that he has no time for orderly management of his staff." Henry agrees that the pressures are unbelievable and conceded that, "I am not doing any one thing as well as I could if I weren't doing anything else." But he insisted, "There is no inconsistency between serving the President and orderly administration. If a conflict arose, I would sacrifice orderly administration. But I have an absolutely first-class staff, and they don't need detailed guidance from me."

The Council is the eyes and ears of the President of the United States: Kissinger has the glasses and earphones. Once in a while those eyes see too much and turn against the boss. Former Kissinger assistants Morton Halperin and Les Gelb are among those who have publicly criticized the White House Security operation.

One of Kissinger's tactics was to have repeated meetings with leading opponents of the Vietnam War. First they were quiet, and then word was leaked to the press. Senator Eugene McCarthy was brought to the White House to lunch with the Presidential adviser and express his views. He was followed by Senator George McGovern, a Catholic nun, a couple of Quakers, some antiwar activists, and even a supposed co-conspirator with the Berrigan brothers. John Gardner, the ·founder of Common Cause, and other luminaries of previous Administrations also received an opportunity to try to move the immovable Kissinger from his position on Vietnam.

Not much came of all this activity. Kissinger was not likely to be influenced by the views of those the President had publicly opposed. Nor were firmly committed anti-Vietnam United States Senators, radical Professors, or former Cabinet members susceptible to friendly persuasion by Kissinger. The Professor can be charming, but he has no magical powers.

✦

CHAPTER 10

J. EDGAR HOOVER

Although Kissinger's title of Presidential Assistant is only for foreign affairs, Nixon uses him as a sounding board and adviser for major domestic decisions, too. Henry does not have the feel for pure politics, but his agile, logical mind can help bridge the gap between inconsistent policies.

Nixon needed all the assistance he could get in the matter of J. Edgar Hoover and Red China.

In 1962 in his book *Six Crises*, Nixon had written: "Admitting Red China to the United Nations would be a mockery of the provisions of the charter which limits its membership to 'Peace-loving nations' . . . it would give respectability to the Communist regime which would immensely increase its power and prestige in Asia, and probably irreparably weaken the non-Communist governments in that area." By the summer of 1971, events had changed his mind, and he needed help in justifying why he'd rather switch than fight.

The late John Edgar Hoover was seventy-four when Nixon became President. He had long before lost his ability to adapt to new problems or points of view. Some people urged that he be forcibly retired. The comedians portrayed him as a senile loner out of touch with everyone and everything except his own FBI. And in many ways they were right.

115

Even Alvin Karpis, one of his better-known ten-most-wanted criminals, had clobbered Hoover in print as a glory-seeker who had "waited in the shadows" until other agents had pinned the master criminal down. Then, he said, Hoover appeared to make the arrest and call a press conference.

Hoover had not paid much attention to Nixon when he was Eisenhower's Vice President. But he was pleased when Nixon beat "the liberal" and got to the White House. He confided to friends that Nixon at least appreciated the threat of international Communism that Hoover had been harping on for decades.

J. Edgar was well sheltered from the winds of change. Hoover's aides made a practice of sifting through the news and bringing only pleasantries to their Director. The world's "top crime fighter" got more than irritable unless he heard exactly what he wanted to. As a result he did not understand consensus politics and often embarrassed the White House.

For a long time Kissinger kept out of the dispute over whether Hoover should be forcibly retired. Privately he was inclined to believe a change was necessary if Nixon was ever to pick up support from young voters. The President had not exactly captured the hearts and minds of the youth with his position on the eighteen-year-old vote: Only when its passage seemed a hopeless reality had he reluctantly gone along with lowering the voting age to eighteen. Young Americans were the voters most offended by Hoover's provincialism, and Nixon could use some of their votes in 1972.

Then J. Edgar goofed—and badly—when Nixon was about to announce his projected trip to Red China. It was a venture dear to the heart of Kissinger, the theoretician and advance man. He had waited more than three years to reactivate the plan he had privately given Governor Nelson Rockefeller for reopening the door to China. Nixon had considered the proposal, wrestled with the decision, and finally acquiesced because of pressure from U.S. Allies and his aspirations for a second term.

Hoover was not among the handful of top officials consulted when plans for the President's visit to China were brewing. FBI aides ignored all the feelers and tips in the papers that a change in China policy was imminent. Hoover didn't know about it. If he had known about it, he wouldn't have understood it. It was hardly surprising, then, that during a routine appearance before a Congressional committee, Hoover routinely warned the lawmakers, "The United States is Communist China's No. 1 enemy. . . . The most potent threat to our national security is Red China."

ZAP!

Kissinger was furious. In a few days the President of the United States would announce his plans to visit the People's Republic of China. Hoover's blunder would hurt in two ways. First, the right wing that still worshiped the tired supercop would be suspicious of Nixon's decision. And, secondly, it would appear to critics that the President was not holding his team together.

Kissinger's top aide and Attorney General Mitchell quietly arranged for the FBI Director's comments not to be published "for budget reasons."

Under six Administrations, Mr. Hoover had been seemingly immune from criticism or interference. He was as much an American institution as apple pie. If any Attorney General or even a President wanted to pick a fight with the unapproachable monarch, he never publicly showed it. Now the nation was hearing the strange sounds of concerted public criticism of Hoover and his organization from Congress, from the press, and from remote corners of the White House. Even the silence vow that had made political monks of FBI agents since 1924 was broken and the damage was showing.

There was plenty of provocation.

Hoover had thrown away the rule book and failed to consult with the Justice Department when he announced in 1970 a "conspiracy of priests." He named the Berrigan brothers, nuns, and radical laymen as the "East Coast Conspiracy to Save Lives." These "traitors to their church and nation" were planning to kidnap Henry Kissinger and make him an international hostage until Nixon pulled out of Vietnam, Hoover said. Two years and a few million dollars later, a jury was hung on that charge. The FBI Director had also warned of a plot to blow up the steampipes underneath Washington, D.C., and create a citywide stopped-up toilet.

It was incredible to have the nation's top cop accuse people of serious crimes before an indictment had been brought. But, he was J. Edgar Hoover—and above the rules.

"We'll be able to snatch the angel some evening when he is alone . . . or maybe we can find out where he shacks up and get him then."

The Justice Department contended these were the words of Roman Catholic Priest Philip Berrigan in a letter to Sister Elizabeth McAlister. The "angel" referred to was obviously Henry, it was reasoned. Who else could most easily be kidnapped when he was getting laid?

The other Father Berrigan was originally charged also. But the second set of indictments from the federal grand jury in Harrisburg, Pennsylvania, dropped Father Daniel Berrigan as a defendant. Along with the alleged plot to kidnap Kissinger and blow up the heating and plumbing tunnels in Washington, the grand jury added charges of conspiracy to steal and destroy Selective Service records.

118

The FBI claimed undercover agents had infiltrated the U.S. Penitentiary at Lewisburg, Pennsylvania, and the various priests, nuns, former clergymen, and laymen were all traitors.

Kissinger did not comment, but the Secret Service doubled the Professor's protection, fearing retaliation for Hoover's charges.

Even more incredible than the alleged plot was Hoover's audacity in publicly charging Berrigan and company before a grand jury did. It created the same sort of furor as when President Nixon appeared to convict Charles Manson of murder before the jury had retired. The screaming headlines, NIXON SAYS MANSON GUILTY, went around the world and were trailed by a hasty explanation and denial from the Presidential Press Secretary. When Hoover made a comparable boner, he did not bother to explain or deny.

In another time, the Sacred Cow in charge of the FBI might have gotten away with it. But not now. The attack was led by Democratic Congressman William R. Anderson of Tennessee. He was no red-eyed screaming liberal. Anderson had been Commander of the atomic submarine *Nautilus* and catapulted his military reputation into a solid political career. Anderson was not alone in refusing to accept Hoover's charges with no evidence offered at the time. Anyone who had a gripe against the FBI suddenly felt free to speak out. It became open season on the Director. Nixon and Kissinger sat back and calmly watched Hoover's stature drop quicker than if they had done the job.

The Majority Leader of the House of Representatives was another Southerner, Representative Hale Boggs of Louisiana. He jumped on the bandwagon and accused Hoover of wiretapping Congressional homes and offices. The FBI denied it vehemently.

The action shifted from the House to the Senate. Senator

Ed Muskie was trying to pick up political support among young voters and environmentalists of every age. He suddenly showed up with an FBI report proving surveillance of Earth Day, the nationwide anti-pollution rally.

The Congressional pièce de résistance was the discovery that Hoover's FBI had sent an undercover informer into Texas Representative John Dowdy's office with a concealed tape recorder.

The journalists who had for years blasted Hoover's machine tactics were picking up more readers and new incidents to report.

A small FBI office in Media, Pennsylvania, was broken into and over 1,000 secret documents were lifted from Hoover's local sanctuary. The raiders had called themselves the Citizens' Commission to Investigate the FBI. The documents were copied and distributed to magazines and newspapers. They proved extensive and expensive FBI investigation and surveillance of Black leaders and campus groups, many of whom had not been involved in anything more reprehensible than disagreeing with the Vietnam War. The Hoover protective coat was cracking.

Although the White House does not have its own full-time intelligence team, it usually gets classified information first. The various government agencies that compete with the FBI are anxious to show up Hoover's agents by passing on a bit of secret news before it funnels to the President from the FBI Director's tower. An Army intelligence officer had learned about an internal problem at the FBI; and he had warned his boss, who in turn told Kissinger's aide, Brigadier General Haig.

An FBI agent named John F. Shaw was enrolled in the graduate program of the John Jay College of Criminal Justice in New York. Shaw was one of several brushing up for an assignment at the FBI's National Police Academy.

He wrote a fifteen-page private letter to one of his instructors in response to a comment in class about the Bureau. Shaw was complimentary about Hoover's personal integrity, but pointed out that certain Bureau policies and procedures were antiquated. The otherwise careful agent made the mistake of asking a girl in the FBI typing pool to type it up. She kept a copy, and it reached Hoover the next day. He was incensed.

The FBI does not waste time on modern concepts like due process when it comes to disciplining its own men. (To give the Devil his due, Hoover forged the most efficient police unit in the world by vigorous strict discipline, right down to the prescribed three-quarter inch for a breast pocket handkerchief to show.) Shaw was suspended for thirty days and transferred to the FBI's Siberia—Butte, Montana. The agent's wife was critically ill, and he refused to go. He told the bureau off and quit.

Senator George McGovern took up Agent Shaw's fight and demanded a Congressional inquiry into Hoover's dictatorial powers and the persecution of this agent. The Presidential aspirant produced an unsigned letter which purported to be from ten other agents supporting Shaw's charges. (This one was not prepared in the typing pool.)

Shaw's story got a happy ending at the Director's expense. He filed suit in federal court charging that he had been the victim of a "capricious and vindictive act of personal retribution" by Hoover. The FBI settled the case, cleaned up Shaw's record, and agreed to pay him $13,000.

Hoover was determined to have the last word, and there was pressure to have Shaw's instructor at John Jay College fired. As a result, the fifteen FBI agents who were enrolled dropped out of the college. That brought more adverse publicity for the FBI Director.

Hoover was already years beyond normal federal retirement age when death took him in the spring of 1972, thus ending speculation that President Nixon would replace him, despite the retirement exemption granted him by LBJ. Hoover probably could have gotten away with the Berrigan goof, the Shaw incident, and even survived the attacks of Anderson, Boggs, Muskie, Dowdie, McGovern, and other Congressional critics. But even J. Edgar Hoover could go too far, and he did when he screwed around with Kissinger's China policy. His days as FBI Director were probably numbered when he died.

CHAPTER 11

—————— ✠ ——————

THE OPPENHEIM AFFAIR

A Fantasy Phone Call
HELLO . . . MISS ST. JOHN? . . . MISS JILL ST. JOHN?
LISTEN, YOU DON'T KNOW ME BUT MY NAME IS
DICK NIXON AND I GOT YOUR TELEPHONE NUMBER
FROM A MUTUAL FRIEND . . .

A Reasonable Hypothesis
If Henry Kissinger spends as much time with women as the
women claim, he hasn't been to his office in years.

Henry Kissinger was a student at George Washington
High School in New York in 1941. Jill Oppenheim was born
in August of that year. The Kissingers of New York didn't
know the Oppenheims of California.

By the time she was four, Jill was the star of her singing
and dancing classes. At age six, she had her first part in a radio
soap opera, and was a child model. Still no one suspected then
that she would grow up deliciously to be Jill St. John, the
movie star, and be romantically linked with leaders of the international jet set like millionaire horseman Ogden Phipps, Jr.,
Italian jeweler Gianni Bulgari, Hollywood's David Wolper,
and the second most powerful man in the government of the
United States—the kid from Washington Heights.

She grew up to be all that. And more.

Mr. and Mrs. Kirk Douglas are among the leaders of the movie set who enjoy bringing together a mixture of show business and political personalities. In between his fourth and fifth secret Vietnam meetings in Paris, Kissinger found time for a Douglas bash at the actor's home.

The best-looking woman there was Jill St. John, on the arm of her former beau Frank Sinatra. Jill's press agents claimed she had a high IQ and was capable of doing a lot more than simply being the All-American Sex Pot. In the 1968 election she had displayed her political convictions by flashing a McCarthy for President button.

Only in America could a kinky-haired, horn-rimmed college professor steal a date from the jet set's unofficial leader, Frank Sinatra. A late date was arranged and a romance was inaugurated. Over the next few months, Jill showed up all over California with Henry, and Henry showed up all over Jill in Washington, D.C. Her low-cut dresses turned on everybody at the Jockey Club and Le Provençal. The happiest guy in Hollywood was publicity agent Richard Gully, who never let a day go by without sending out a press release touting the relationship between Jill and the Presidential adviser.

Kissinger has the unique ability to invite a good-looking woman to a particular event and suddenly forget the invitation when the press finds out. In one case, the World Cup soccer matches were to be held in Mexico City with all of the royal banners unfurled. Kissinger was going, not only as a Presidential delegate but as an ardent soccer fan who had been a pretty good kicker back in Germany. Press agent Gully jumped the gun by sending out a press release announcing that Jill St. John would accompany Dr. Kissinger to Mexico City for the opening ceremony. Kissinger quickly denied it, and there was a ridiculous amount of fuss over who was going where with whom when not very many people really cared.

Jill St. John is a character out of a Harold Robbins novel. Men want to share her vicariously. Her clothes and cosmetics and jewelry and cars and home and cockiness are enough to shake up anybody. Kissinger, who had previously established himself as a political mountain climber, couldn't help but respond to the well-endowed Miss St. John.

The only other politician whom Jill had ever gotten close to was Lieutenant Governor Benjamin Barnes of Texas, whose conservative supporters urged him not to be seen with the flaming redhead in his home state. He didn't listen.

Jill was not unknown in California political circles. She was a leader of the anti-Nixon forces on the West Coast. When the President took up his summer White House at San Clemente, she was quoted by the wire services as commenting that "Nixon living in Orange County (the most reactionary part of the state) was most fitting."

While Kissinger was interested in Jill's physical attributes, she wanted to talk about the war in Vietnam. An active pacifist, she clobbered Henry at their first meeting for his association with the war. Her tone changed, however, when reporters questioned her later that week about her relationship with Nixon's Number Two man. By then, he had become "brilliant, thoughtful, kind, generous, and lovely."

Jill either had some excellent pre-Kissinger speech writers or her reputed high IQ exists. She had told a local California paper her views on the Nixon Administration in terms that many a Democratic candidate would like to have thought of. "I have heard about the Spiro Agnew watch . . . you wind it up and it ticks like a bomb. I don't mean to sound like an isolationist, but we had better clean up our house before it gets so

125

dirty the only way to clean it up is to burn it down. . . . I'm on the side of the kids. I believe in what they say. If only people would listen to them. But there is no way . . . they have a moratorium in Washington and Martha Mitchell calls them Communists."

It is not altogether unusual for a Hollywood star to mix kinky clothes and political astuteness. Jill's success on the screen has left her enough time to do more reading, traveling, and politicking than most women in their early thirties.

In 1958 while Kissinger was writing an article on "Missiles and the Western Alliance," Jill married Neil Dubin, a laundry heir. It lasted one month. Spouse Number Two was the late Lance Reventlow, the playboy son of Barbara Hutton and heir to the Woolworth fortune. That marriage didn't last long either. When she accepted a $100,000 property settlement in getting out of the Reventlow marriage, she told reporters, "I don't believe in alimony if you work. . . . But a property settlement's okay!"

In 1967, when Kissinger was getting ready to go to work for Nelson Rockefeller at his combination Foundation-political headquarters, Jill was marrying singer Jack Jones. Can you believe it . . . Jack and Jill Jones? Any couple with names like that must be destined to climb up the hill of matrimony and come tumbling down. They did. It became a classic Hollywood relationship, with the marriage a total failure and the divorce a great success.

According to Maxine Cheshire of the *Washington Post* (June 19, 1970), after her romance with Kissinger began, Jill became offended when the press compared her to George Hamilton, who was said to have milked his association with President Johnson's daughter, Lynda Bird. Jill said her relationship with Henry was based upon intellectual things, like discussing world events and playing chess. "I enjoy playing with Henry Kissinger much more than Sean Connery. . . . I don't know why. He's just more fun to play with," Jill told a fan magazine writer about her chess game.

One embarrassing event for Miss St. John occurred when a subpoena was issued for her in the United States District Court in New York in connection with the criminal trial of Nathan Voloshen and Martin Sweig, who were charged with using House of Representatives Speaker John W. McCormack's office for bribery. Although the subpoena was never served, the judge read the names of Miss St. John and eighty-one other individuals who were involved in the testimony concerning Sweig.

Jill St. John always contends that a girl wants to be known for her accomplishments, not just her looks. When she sits opposite the Professor at Chasen's, some of her accomplishments are obvious. She is the ultimate sex symbol, and among those paying homage is the gentleman from Germany.

✠

CHAPTER 12

DICK AND PAT AND
HENRY AND ZSA ZSA

"I am a marvelous housekeeper. Every time I leave a man, I keep his house."

—ZSA ZSA GABOR in *How to Catch a Man, Keep a Man, and Get Rid of a Man* (1971)

Zsa Zsa told me she'd like to marry Henry Kissinger. "But he will never marry me, Dahling. . . . He thinks I am too much woman for him!"

When Mr. and Mrs. President of the United States entertain on the West Coast, they traditionally decorate their formal state dinners with a cross-section of show-world personalities selected to dazzle their guests. When Dick and Pat set up a dinner in San Francisco honoring the Korean Premier in 1969, they reached out for the California regulars, including former actor Governor Ronald Reagan and former Democrat Frank Sinatra. Then they needed female attractions. No woman in the West offers more tinsel than Zsa Zsa Gabor, who travels bejeweled and befurred like a younger Mae West with accent seasoning. Zsa Zsa was added to the guest list.

The White House Social Secretary telephoned the Gabor Bel Air mansion to invite Zsa Zsa to dinner, and Francesca

Gabor Hilton, the actress daughter of Zsa Zsa and Conrad Hilton, answered. (She usually does. The Hilton heiress is generally available between roles.) But Francesca wasn't invited to the Nixon's dinner. Zsa Zsa was to come alone because of a "very special seating plan" thought up by the President.

Gabor had mixed emotions. She never misses going anywhere to steal the limelight. But she travels with a full entourage, including Mother (the Countess Jolie Gabor), daughter Francesca, her agent, her public relations consultant, her male secretary, her escort, and her hairdresser. A compromise was agreed upon. The Hungarian-born superstar would be permitted one escort. She chose a good-looking Los Angeles lawyer, but he was required to sit in the back of the hall while Zsa Zsa rated the dais.

Zsa Zsa never suspected that President Nixon and his wife were giggling over their having "set up" Henry Kissinger. The Administration's resident lover was being publicized as a super-stud always in the company of young Hollywood fillies. This time they had imported an experienced thoroughbred— Zsa Zsa Gabor.

The Chief of Protocol nearly flipped worrying about the head-table mismatch. How could Nixon's trusted egghead tolerate three hours of "dahling"? Kissinger was an expert on nuclear power, world crises, and our political future. Zsa Zsa's interests supposedly ranged from her cosmetics company to Tiffany's and back again. How could the duo survive the night? But the Protocol Chief was wrong. They got along great! Mainly because, besides her beauty, Zsa Zsa is one of the brightest Hollywood stars.

"He's not much to look at at first but, after he opens his mouth, he's Cary Grant . . . he's everything a woman could want," Zsa Zsa bubbled later. She was thoroughly taken by the man, even though at first she had no idea who he was, she says.

After the dinner a uniformed Marine delivered a message from the President simply asking, "What do you think of my Mr. Kissinger?"

Zsa Zsa wrote back on a napkin, "Who is Mr. Kissinger?"

The reply came from the President, pointing with a little arrow in his own inimitable doodle, "The man in the next chair you've been flirting with all evening!"

Determined to find out what a Henry Kissinger was, Zsa Zsa did her homework. She was impressed and very much interested. The next few months were filled with long-distance calls from Henry to Zsa Zsa and Zsa Zsa to Henry. She consulted him over lunch, dinner, theater, and "after." Her only complaint was "that damn beeper goes off at the wrong time . . . that's how the President calls him . . . always at the wrong time!"

Henry found Zsa Zsa refreshingly bright after his tours of duty with the gushy starlet set. It seemed that every time his friends in Hollywood fixed him up, his dates' boobs got bigger and their brains got smaller (June Wilkinson and Henry Kissinger???). At least, Zsa Zsa was well traveled and well read, and she even shared the Kissinger middle-European mannerisms. As time went by, the Secret Service allowed Henry to see Zsa Zsa without a protective escort. After all, how much trouble could one guy get into in a seven-bedroom house with the world's sexiest mother?

After their second meeting, Zsa Zsa adopted Henry as her personal social protégé. Naturally, she would start with his wardrobe. (Gabor had the habit of bluntly advising all the men she met on color combinations, suit cuts, fabrics, and ties.) The President's aide needed to swing out and balance his conservative, curly-headed, horn-rimmed look, she decreed. Zsa Zsa decided on happy colors in the brown family and urged Henry on to her former beau's exclusive Beverly Hills mandashery—Ron Postal's. The Professor never got around to buying a "today" wardrobe.

There was a certain vivid pattern also in the Kissinger-Gabor telephone romance. Zsa Zsa would say something clever on the Tonight Show and Kissinger would call within minutes after the show's airing to congratulate her. Then Kissinger would rate another news magazine cover, and Zsa Zsa would be on the phone that day, cajoling, kidding, and inviting.

I remember one memorable occasion when Zsa Zsa evoked all of Kissinger's formidable diplomatic powers. We were preparing for a two-week journey from the Bel Air mainland to Hawaii. It was the eve of Zsa Zsa's return to the night-club stage, and we were to break in her new Las Vegas show—which I produced. Preparation for the journey reminded me of the Allied forces getting ready to land at Normandy. At last our party was ready to leave for the airport in a fleet of limousines. There were the Countess (Mama Jolie, who was destined to do a song and dance with Don Ho on stage at Duke Kahanamoku's); Carl, the male secretary; the hairdresser; the public relations lady, whose job was really to sell Zsa Zsa's new line of cosmetics to Liberty House; daughter Francesca; comedian Sandy Baron with his manager; writer-actor John Amos; Tommy Boyce and Bobby Hart—Zsa Zsa's co-stars; some miscellaneous dancers; my assistants; and me. The last member of this entourage was to be Zsa Zsa's Siamese cat.

I gave her the bad news: Cats could not be taken to Hawaii unless they were quarantined for two weeks. Zsa Zsa became furious, declaring that, when she went, her pets went, too. Convinced of the high-level nature of her problem, she grabbed the phone and called the White House. She was able to reach Henry Kissinger faster to meet her crisis than most foreign diplomats could. I am positive that his handling of that call should have won him a Nobel Peace Prize. Somehow, he did the impossible and convinced Zsa Zsa that Hawaii was entitled to have laws regulating the interstate traffic of cats. Miraculously he soothed her and promised to attend her Las Vegas opening night, and all was well.

When Zsa Zsa returned to Las Vegas for her gala opening night, she reminded Kissinger of his promise to attend. The hotel's publicity people jubilantly evisioned Conrad Hilton and Henry A. Kissinger in a photograph taken at ringside, with the label, "the past and the future of Zsa Zsa Gabor."

But Henry didn't show. He just sent roses. It took two years for Zsa Zsa and entourage to learn that, on the day she opened at the Flamingo Hotel, Henry was in a meeting. He was in Paris, trying to end somebody's war.

Alas, the chances of a Kissinger-Gabor nuptial ceremony are just about nil. He still likes the younger stuff! If matrimony for Henry Kissinger was the goal of the matchmakers in the White House, they'll have to try again.

CHAPTER 13

--------- ✠ ---------

MY NAME IS JUDY...
COLOR ME BROWN

A Fantasy White House Bulletin
Subject: Films for White House Library
   Presidential Adviser Henry Kissinger has announced a more liberal policy in the selection of White House films. In an effort to better understand our Scandinavian friends, the X-rated Danish classic Threesome, featuring Judy Brown, will be shown to mature government officials at midnight tonight. (Come stag.)

   Does Nixon know Henry is seeing an X-rated starlet? Who is Judy Brown and why are they saying those things about her? So asked the fan magazines a few months ago when Judy (Color Me Brown) made her Kissinger debut.
   The well-stacked starlet was claiming an intimate acquaintance with Nixon's Henry. The Professor was admitting a little but denying more. The lady, he suggested, was a "publicity maniac." He claimed their torrid love scenes were only played on her press agent's typewriter.
   Judy allowed that she couldn't believe the good doctor would ever say such nasty things, because "he's too fine a gentleman." Besides, he was supposed to be passionately fond of her.

Judging by Kissinger's more recent taste in women, Judy's story was believable. It was told in embarrassing detail in one of the less lurid movie magazines in an article entitled "Starlet Describes Secret Dates with Henry Kissinger." Her physical qualifications seem to meet Henry's standards. According to fan magazines, she's five feet four, with brown eyes, and the standard sheaf of hair falling loosely below her shoulders. Her hair is not called brown in print. . . . It is "mahogany." Her body is great. Her breasts resemble the caricatures in all those dirty little books. Her clothes point up their beauties. Henry prefers her to look that way, she implies. "Henry is always telling me how sexy I am. He appreciates it when I dress up, which I make a point of doing." Her cheekbones are high, and most of her publicity photos show her with a wet, welcoming smile fastened to her face. She invites observers to turn on readily.

Judy may have come to Kissinger's attention as one-third of the orgy in the Danish porno film, *Threesome*. The Customs Department confiscated and then released prints in this country. Now she has moved up to classics like *Women in Cages* and *The Big Doll House*.

How often and with what degree of seriousness Judy and Henry date or swing is hard to say. Her charges and his countercharges don't mix. But no one denies he's been closer than the front row.

According to Henry, the Brown affair lasted for three dinner dates. According to Judy Brown, the Kissinger affair stretched over an entire year with gifts and promises. Judy had been traveling the usual route—from Miss University of Missouri to Beverly Hills, with a cinematic stopover in Denmark. Just before she met Henry, she divorced her jock-turned-salesman mate Jerry Crumpler. She fired her agent. She quit Universal Studios. She was at very loose ends, and determined to make it as a "serious" actress. Then one day, "I got a call from Taft Schreiver, saying that Henry Kissinger was due in town and would I have dinner with him." After finding out who Kissinger was, she agreed to this suggestion.

"A week later the phone rang and it was Henry calling from the White House." Would she have dinner with him— say, Friday night? "I said yes before I even thought what I was saying, and as soon as I hung up I was sorry I had accepted. What in the world was I going to say to Henry Kissinger?"

Judy's agent was soon turning out the hot news of a Kissinger-Brown romance, but it didn't go very far. She was simply another in a long procession of (mostly) figures to be seen with Kissinger. It would take more than a press release to get anybody's attention.

What finally worked was Judy's charges that Kissinger had been keeping her "in a closet" while publicly entertaining more acceptable women like Jill St. John and Marlo Thomas. It's understandable. After all, the man needs intellectual companionship too. What everyone wondered was whether a poor Jewish boy from Manhattan armed with horn-rims and a doctorate could satisfy the needs of an X-rated starlet.

According to Judy, the problem of privacy has been present since their first date. She had cheerfully put up with the anonymity for Henry's sake—a sacrifice that for an aspiring actress is tougher than giving up food. Then one night, Henry took her to the Bistro, in Beverly Hills, for a quiet dinner. Everything was going smoothly—they even received a complimentary bottle of wine. William Wyler stopped by to chat. According to Judy, "Henry is very charmed by this. I think you might say Henry is very charmed by everyone and everything in Hollywood. He loves the glamour." A garrulous

137

waiter remembers the President's adviser as the man with a smile that only comes when there's activity under the table. Apparently Henry was being manipulated.

While Judy was in the ladies' room, a Secret Service agent approached Kissinger with the bad news that a battery of photographers had mysteriously appeared in front of the restaurant. "That's all I need," Kissinger is supposed to have groaned. And so Judy, Kissinger, and the agents made a quick exit through the kitchen and into the alley. Once outside, Judy is reported to have shouted, "Tell me this. If you don't like publicity, then why do you go out with stars?"

According to one account, Kissinger's answer had four letters.

Back at Judy's apartment, she told Kissinger that he couldn't have his cake and eat it too. This suggested one of the most fascinating and sensual options of Kissinger's distinguished career.

She told him that if they were going to continue to see one another they had to stop evading questions about the relationship and stop running out of back doors away from photographers.

Walking to the door, Henry made it all as brief as possible. "Well then," he said, "I guess I won't have my cake."

After a good night's sleep and a conference with her press agent, Judy decided to give a lengthy interview explaining how hurt she was about being "the silent one" in Kissinger's life. "I've done everything in my power," she contended, "to play down our relationship, even to barefaced denials to specific questions about our dating. And Henry has appreciated my discretion. I know this.

"But now I've had it. I've got an ego, too, and he's got to realize that it hurts my feelings to see him written about all over the place with other women. Especially when I *know* they don't mean anything to him, like Margaret Osmer, like Marlo Thomas. He went out with her too. He didn't even know what she did! She said she worked in television and he said 'What do you do?' like maybe she was a secretary. The next day their picture was plastered all over the newspapers. It's been coming out in magazines. A million people are talking about Henry Kissinger and Marlo Thomas and THAT HURTS. I'm tired of being the silent one in his life, the mystery girl."

The interview took care of all that. Within several days Judy's picture was making national papers, everything from the slick news magazines to the confidential crap. The last straw, Judy confided, was the "Margaret Osmer thing." A photo of Kissinger and Osmer, a blonde producer working for CBS-TV, made the front page of the *Los Angeles Times*. She was Henry's respectable cover during one of his early secret Paris trips.

Judy started wearing a new type of nail polish—a deep, blood-red. She called it, she said, Kissinger Red.

Not only did Judy tell all, she added some color and began forecasting their future. Henry would return, she claimed. He had already promised that they would "go to every restaurant in town and let photographers take all the pictures they want." Supposedly, at that point the photographers would leave. Henry obviously wasn't ready for Denmark.

Kissinger's first remarks about some meager exposé had to do with the incident at the Bistro. Who, he wondered, could have called all those photographers in? He didn't, and the restaurant wouldn't, so that left—. Then the President's man began escalating his remarks—from question to rebuke. They had, he said, dated "only three times." Unfortunately, several gossip columnists fell upon the remark, and readily provided a list of the places Kissinger and Judy had been seen together.

The list included Kissinger's house at San Clemente, a locale in Palm Springs, and such Hollywood hangouts as Chasen's, and the Bistro.

So Henry escalated again—from rebuke to mad denial. Then he left for China, safe in international negotiations, relieved of the necessity for personal defense. After all, it was a very small secret romance and he *was* a secret agent.

After the "publicity maniac" remark, Judy acknowledged she was sick of the entire matter. "It's a whole other thing when you open up the paper and see it in your own backyard," she gulped. And that was that.

The Judy Brown case history presents some interesting insights into the options open to Henry Kissinger and his ladies. The way of it is that, if you accept a date with Henry Kissinger, you can probably trade on his name. Kissinger knows that better than anyone else. He's not unwilling to barter. He apparently always gets what he wants, and so do his dates. Probably the girls use him. If they do it subtly, well, why not? And if they become carried away—drunk with newsprint—a denial will set things right.

It can only enhance his studhood to be seen with so many remarkable women, and that attracts more. If he declines comment on them, he becomes the courtly gentleman, the cavalier who doesn't tell. Of course, if he's been had, he dons his role as Presidential adviser, and loses himself in the dignity and secrecy of his office. How, says innocent Henry, can these women stoop so to trade on his name? However it happens, the Kissinger myth keeps getting built. And his dates keep getting builter.

CHAPTER 14

———— ✠ ————

MARLO THOMAS

A Fantasy Investigation Report
N *HENRY, I WANT YOU TO QUIETLY FIND OUT
   WHAT THE ARABS THINK OF MY MIDDLE-EAST
   POLICY.*
K *But, Mr. President, I don't know any Arabs.*
N *FIND ONE!*

Subject: Marlo Thomas

The subject was the latest of a bevy of Hollywood stars (but first TV type) to break bread with Dr. K. Earlier reports that Hollywood executive Taft Schreiver was responsible for this match have not been confirmed. Schreiver has, however, been identified as the advance man for Kissinger with Judy Brown.

According to the *Los Angeles Times* of April 7, 1971, among those who appeared at Chasen's Restaurant on the night in question and stopped to speak to Kissinger and companion were American Broadcasting Company President Leonard Goldenson (see Confidential Presidential Report on Suspicious TV Network Officials), and Paul Keyes, who writes for Laugh-In. Keyes was in the company of the aforesaid Schreiver, who was permitted to approach Dr. K.'s table because of his previous affiliation as Ronald Reagan's associate in *Death Valley Days*.

The day after the night at Chasen's, agents began circulating pictures and biographies of Miss Thomas to various studios, pointing out, "She isn't under contract to anyone at the moment and is looking for roles that are more serious than what she has done before."

United Press International has reported that Miss Thomas was the brunette spotted jogging with Dr. K. on San Clemente Beach outside the Western White House the previous weekend.

Although Miss Thomas was born in Detroit, Michigan, in 1938, she is not known to be involved with any questionable labor organizations. Miss Thomas was sired by noted Lebanese entertainer, Danny Thomas, was given birth by his wife, Rosemary, and was raised in Los Angeles, California. She attended a Beverly Hills Catholic Grammar School and Marymount High School. (There is no evidence of any involvement with the Berrigans or other radical religious leaders, despite her parochial training.)

It should be noted, however, that Miss Thomas did appear in a television series *77 Sunset Strip*, which escaped government censors. (See Presidential Report on Pornographic Titles and Obscene Labels.) Her ethnic sympathies were apparent from her role in a summer stock show in Santa Barbara, California, entitled *Black Chiffon*.

After performances in California-based television shows, including *Ben Casey, Mr. Novak, The Virginian,* and *Bonanza,* Miss Thomas achieved recognition as the lead in *Barefoot in the Park* (an English production directed by questionably radical director Mike Nichols).

Miss Thomas is a member of the Board of Directors of the so-called Inner-City Cultural Center, a so-called interracial so-called non-profit professional theater headed by so-called actor Gregory Peck. (Peck has been under continuous surveillance since his participation in a heavily anti-anti-Semitic motion picture, *Gentleman's Agreement,* many years ago.)

Her most suspect association is "Neighbors of Watts," a so-called building plan designed to develop so-called child-care centers in the Watts neighborhood of Los Angeles. No substantive evidence has linked Miss Thomas with the Watts disturbances yet.

Reliable sources indicate her motives do not represent a threat to the security of the United States, and bugging will probably not be necessary. Dr. K. has, however, received the Anti-Mata Hari Dissemination of Vital Information Capsule, which will keep him patriotically impotent for twenty-four hours.

Miss Thomas resides in a large structure behind wrought-iron gates on three and a half acres of the most expensive land in Beverly Hills.

Miss Thomas's former sorority housemother, Clemmy, is at the University of Southern California, and has recollections of Marlo's pledgeship, membership, and Vice Presidency of Delta Theta sorority. (There is no evidence of radical campus disturbances at that time involving the surveillee.) Miss Thomas earned a primary teaching credential, and with highest recommendations proceeded to break a contract with the Beverly Hills School District.

The person most responsible for her change from ordinariness is Dr. Morey Parks, the six-figure-a-year plastic surgeon, 9201 Sunset Drive, Hollywood, who performed her nose operation, enabling her to become "That Girl" and dine with Dr. K.

Miss Thomas has confided to friends that she finds Mr. Kissinger "terribly charming, extremely intelligent, and lovely company." She has specifically indicated that there is no marriage or engagement in the offing. It is significant to note that no one has ever suggested that there was, and yet she has continually denied same.

A more thorough discussion of Miss Thomas's activities with Dr. K. may be obtained by subpoenaing private files of one Rona Barrett of California, confidante of the stars and soothsayer of sexual and social synthetics in Hollywood.

CHAPTER 15

✠

STEINEM v. KISSINGER

"Gloria Steinem is not now and has never been my girl friend. But I am not discouraged. After all, she did not say that if nominated, she would not accept or if elected, she would not serve."
—HENRY A. KISSINGER at "Salute to Congress" dinner (quoted in *Newsweek*, February 7, 1972)

By the time a boy has been laid twice, he is convinced he is an expert. He can then devote his free time to fantasizing about a magical list of girls he would like to be with. He can start with the best-looking cheerleader, no matter how tough her football hero-boy friend is, and he can even add the older woman at the drive-in. Nobody is hurt, because he usually doesn't share that fantasy with anyone except a few close buddies in the locker room while changing for a high-school gym class.

When he grows a little older, he continues to fantasize. And he broadens his scope to include the wife of a good friend or business associate and the movie starlet that his wife "can't see" but that he would love to bed down with.

The bigger the star, the greater the challenge. Even Joe Namath's critics will not deny a little bit of jealous admiration

145

when they see him escorting Raquel Welch to the Academy Awards in Hollywood. A man can almost rise above politics when he visualizes Henry Kissinger running around town with Jill St. John, Judy Brown, Marlo Thomas, or some other beauty that he has fantasized about. Truly Kissinger has a magical list. Obviously the Professor likes a challenge too.

Ms. Gloria Steinem is indeed a toothsome and formidable challenge.

At a small midwestern college a few months ago, a poll was taken to determine who the students felt were the most important Americans of our time. Gloria Steinem beat out Ralph Nader for Number One by over sixty votes, despite the fact that the school has a predominantly male population. These are the times of change, but the poll results were not necessarily a victory for Women's Lib. The challenge may be a little different, but the desire is the same.

It was a front-page news story when Gloria Steinem declared, "I am not now, nor have I ever been, the girl friend of Henry Kissinger." The emphatic denial was repeated by Kissinger, but to some it seemed there was added a wistful ray of hope.

When traditional male chauvinist reporters began covering Women's Liberation Day gatherings in New York, more than one would comment, "I'd like to liberate that," when they spotted Gloria. She is probably less in need of any kind of salvation than any other woman of the world. Highly educated, with what even women describe as a perfect body, Gloria is a beauty right down to her four-inch heels and braless clinging T-shirt. At thirty-five, she can boast not only of having a Bachelor's degree in government, magna cum laude, from Smith College, but of having been a fellow at the University of Delhi and the University of Calcutta in India.

Equally important, Gloria Steinem's work has been pub-

146

lished in many major magazines, including *Esquire, Life, Harper's, Vogue, Glamour, New York Times, McCall's, Ladies' Home Journal,* and *Show.* She shares the mantle of leadership in the Women's Liberation Movement with only three others —Congresswoman Bella Abzug, Congresswoman Shirley Chisholm, and Betty Friedan; and by God, she is by far the most woman of the four!

Gloria Steinem was born in Toledo, Ohio, as a second daughter of an itinerant Jewish antique dealer who split up with her mother when she was eleven. Her grandmother, Ruth Steinem, was a suffragette and a newspaper woman. The part of Ohio that she grew up in is known as "Joe" country, where they beat up the first available Black on Saturday night just for something to do. She well remembers, "We were considered nuts on two counts: We read books and we were poorer than they were. The girls all got married before they graduated because they were pregnant.

"I had one girl friend like that with four children too fast. Her teeth fell out. Now she sits at home and her husband beats her from time to time for recreation."

You do not have to be Black to know poverty, and Gloria Steinem's home was as bad as her neighborhood. After the divorce, her mother had no income; and they lived literally in a rat-filled slum. "Gloria would wake up at night and pull her toes in underneath her so they wouldn't be bitten off by rats," her mother told one magazine reporter.

When she was fifteen years old, she moved to Washington, D.C.; and in that "glorious city," she became a real teenager with her twenty-five-year-old sister looking over. It was a whole new world of people who sat down to eat at decent hours, did not have to stand in line to go to the john, and would not look strangely at you for reading a book. Gloria was a lousy student, not because she did not have the brains, but

147

because she was too poor and too busy to develop any decent study habits. But her college board exams came along, and raw intellect showed through and popped her into Smith College.

Her mother sold the house, her only asset, to pay the bills of that overpriced institution, while Gloria continued her assault on the beautiful new world. She was at the top of her class in political science, but she really had not begun to make herself heard until she got her fellowship to India.

Her comments made sense about this country to women and men alike. "America is an enormous frosted cupcake in the middle of millions of starving people," she says now. "I discovered that I'd been ghetto-ized as a white person—there were no Black girls at Smith, for example—and in retrospect I was furious. I came home filled with a crusading zeal to make this country aware of what was going on in Asia."

One of the more astute political writers on the West Coast compared Gloria's experiences in India with those of Angela Davis in France. Both came from relatively low-income families and got their first taste of revolution outside this country. Both were highly educated and had a flair for teaching and speaking. One got involved in a more activist vein than the other and stood trial for her life. The other is considered a super-chick among the jet setters, and the woman many would most like to make it with.

Ironically, she took a job in New York for the CIA-funded National Student Association when it was busy posting American kids to Communist-run youth festivals in Europe. She could write, and she got a few assignments from *Esquire* in 1961. Then she took the journalism field by storm at the age of twenty-six with a tremendous article about the pill called "The Moral Disarmament of Betty Coed."

The article was no prize winner as far as writing style is concerned, but within it was a remarkable prophecy. She predicted that, "The real danger of the contraceptive revolution may be the acceleration of woman's role change without any corresponding change of man's attitude toward her role." This was somewhat of a keynote to the women's revolution of which she was to become so very much a part.

She earned a reputation among the editors in New York for being able to spot a trend quickly, and was given key assignments to write about the stalled campaigns of Senator Eugene McCarthy for President and New York Congressman Richard Ottinger for U.S. Senator. On occasion, she blew it. She wrote that Conservative-Republican James Buckley could never muster the support to get elected Senator in New York. He is serving in the United States Senate today.

As a result of her "Betty Coed" article, Gloria got an assignment from *Show* Magazine to infiltrate that unique group of women known as the family of bunnies at the New York Playboy Club. She applied, was accepted and trained as a bunny, and invaded the Club, sticking around long enough to put together a devastating exposé of her experience. Playboy tycoon Hugh Hefner is still galled at her gall.

Show Magazine carried "A Bunny's Tale" in two parts in 1963, and the theatrical rights were quickly purchased by David Merrick for a potential musical. Gloria had answered a classified ad, using the name Marie Ochs. She survived two bunny interviews. She even sat through the bunny lectures, read her funny bunny bible, was fitted for funny bunny eyelashes, and then spent three weeks having her tail tweaked. Her recollections of the first night were "hysterical."

"The bunny room was chaotic and jammed with the usual assortment of girls in high heels and little else. I was pushed and tugged and zipped into my electric-blue costume by the wardrobe mistress, but this time she allowed me to stuff my own bosom."

149

She revealed the strange doctor's exam that all rabbiteers take. " 'This is the part the girls hate,' said the pink-skinned doctor and took blood from my arm for a Wassermann test. I told him that testing for venereal disease seemed a little ominous. 'Don't be silly,' he said, 'all the employees have to do it. You'll know everyone in the club is clean.' 'Okay,' I said, 'I have to have a Wassermann. But what about an internal examination? Is that required of waitresses in New York State?' 'What do you care?' he said. 'It's free and it's for everybody's good. Look, we usually find that girls who object to it strenuously have some reason. . . .' "

The part of the article that really bugged Hugh Hefner was the revelation that the cloakroom girls do not get to keep their tips—these go to the bartenders or the managers or the boss. Also he was far from happy with her charge that the hours were ridiculously long and the pay ridiculously short.

The style of her exposé was more that of a reforming labor leader than a woman's liberator. Nowhere did Gloria suggest that the plight of the poor bunny had anything to do with her being the traditional female sex object. Evidently her revolutionary consciousness was still lying dormant.

Suddenly Gloria Steinem was exploding all over the country as a writer on pop culture, superstars in entertainment, and the Kennedys. Her social life was flourishing, as a wide variety of New Frontiersmen, New York executives, athletes, and movie stars discovered that beneath that beautiful and gutsy front there was a super-chick.

Gloria now lives in an East Side apartment in New York with a décor that combines pop art and affectionately autographed pictures of everyone from César Chávez to Bobby Kennedy. On a typical afternoon she will be speech-writing and the phone will ring—it's Senator Ted Kennedy. Then the phone rings again and it's Senator George McGovern. Again, and it's Mayor John Lindsay. In politics today nobody can ignore the successful femme fatale.

When Gloria first hit New York, she went to work for Harvey Kurtzman at a struggling magazine called *HELP*. The magazine was desperately in need of people to appear on its covers. Gloria's job was to turn on all the big shots and get them to say yes. More of a tribute to her female movements than her female liberation movements was her success in getting Sid Caesar, Jonathan Winters, Jackie Gleason, Mort Sahl, and Milton Berle (Gloria never recommended any woman for the cover).

Kurtzman even decided to play high-level Cupid and dreamed up the perfect match for Gloria—Hugh Hefner. "Both had this thing with the opposite sex. Both depended on the opposite sex for their careers. At the same time, both had never really committed themselves to anybody for anything." This was Kurtzman's philosophy when he arranged a party in Hefner's honor at a photographer's studio, and Gloria promised to come.

Kurtzman remembers the night as being "very glamorous, with all the stupid, skinny, flat-chested model types." Gloria didn't show. She was in the middle of her secret agent work as a Playboy bunny and was afraid that meeting Hefner might give away the whole thing.

She didn't meet her male counterpart until ten years later when she interviewed him for *McCall's* Magazine. Instead of an interview, she ended up telling him off, saying that his crusade for sexual liberation was "beating a dead horse."

"So," sighs Kurtzman, "they never got married and both lived happily ever after."

When Tom Guinzburg, President of Viking Press, picked up the rights to Gloria's book, *The Beach Book* (published in 1963), he also picked up certain rights to Gloria. "I won't say we were exactly Scott and Zelda," the publisher says, "but we were very cute together." The activist publisher was able to convince John Kenneth Galbraith to write an introduction for Gloria's book. They met on Long Island to discuss the project, and Gloria put aside her liberationist tendencies and Guinzburg long enough to fall in love.

The book sold very few copies, but Gloria met almost everybody who was anybody in publishing. Galbraith is still a close, close friend and adviser.

Now it was time for the ambitious chick to make her political move. She decided on the Kennedy team and moved in on Ted Sorensen, the somewhat naïve alter ego of the late President John F. Kennedy. Her political views had very little to do with her appeal. She's a sexy broad, and after you get beyond the first view of the Steinem charm, she's even more complicated than the average beautiful female.

Sorensen was a square and didn't want her to drink or smoke. He told her to wear her hair in a bun and be more feminine. You can't get any more feminine than Gloria Steinem, no matter what she says. After a short time, Sorensen was "out of office."

Today, Gloria could pass for what some of her fellow liberationists call the stereotype of the eternal female sex object. She wears a pair of "skin-tight hip-hugging razzberry levis, two-inch wedgies, and a tight T-shirt, with long blonde hair falling just above each breast." She looks halfway between a University of Michigan cheerleader and the best-looking hustler you've ever seen.

She has become in a very short time the unquestioned spokeswoman for the Women's Liberation Movement. The Movement labels Kissinger as right next to John Wayne among undesirables. She's the one who is sought after as a fund-raiser, speech-maker, and prime missionary to the heathen men. She also becomes a mediator in disputes, and is political adviser to her buddies Congresswomen Shirley Chisholm and Bella Abzug. Together they formed, with Betty Friedan of the National Organization for Women, the National Women's Political Caucus in 1971. Its purpose was to get women and women's issues a full partnership in the American political scene. In order to do it, men like Kissinger would have to listen.

If you could poll the men who have known Gloria, few of them would think she's above or below bedding down with anybody or everybody to achieve the goals of her campaign. But sometimes the tease can do more than the deed. She turned on Kissinger and he reacted—or overreacted—by indicating to the press that she was someone he was interested in. She blasted him publicly for being pushy and, when they did finally get together, it had to be done with mutually agreed secrecy.

The reason that Gloria Steinem has been so successful as a liberationist is simply that she did not have to be. The butchy muscle-bound chicks who one time invaded the Dick Cavett show, and go around the country turning off anybody who might otherwise listen, are not her ilk. This is a good-looking woman who could have made it in education with her mind, or in fashion with her body. But she has chosen the Women's Liberation Movement for her efforts, and she is doing one whale of a job. She has become known on four continents and has had opportunities to turn down the best television talk shows. Her boy friends have gone the gamut from actor-director Mike Nichols to Black Olympic star Rafer Johnson and playwright Herb Sargent. More important than suitors are her close buddies ranging from Senator George McGovern to all of the Kennedys that are still around, and to César Chávez and his group.

"Now I feel I'm doing something nobody else can do," she says. "If someone else can do it, then it's not for me. And so much of what women do—being a secretary, doing housework—they are always made to feel like an interchangeable moving part."

Some of the critics who just cannot accept her as part of any kind of Women's Liberation Movement are the ones who continually say, "I'd like to liberate that myself." They still shake their heads when she gives off the party line. "If you don't want to be a sex object, you have to make yourself unattractive," she complains, "but I'm not going to walk around in Army boots and cut off my hair. There's no reason for us to make ourselves look like men." From a practical standpoint nobody would listen to an Army-booted bald Gloria Steinem, but in her present posture she can get in to see almost anybody.

She has been paired with a dozen or so civil rights-oriented speakers and usually ends up on the podium with her close friend, Dorothy Pitman Hughes, who pioneered New York's day-care program. Her honorarium is just a few hundred dollars, as compared to Al Capp's $3,000 talks spewing "conservative crap." But she is tremendously in demand.

When the columnists started talking about the possibility of a Steinem-Kissinger romance, the inevitable question of how a Women's Lib leader feels about marriage came up. For Gloria marriage is a dubiety. "I may get married some day, but not in the conventional sense I used to think of," she recently said. "Marriage makes you half a person, and what man wants to live with half a person?"

Kissinger probably first became acutely aware of Ms. Steinem as a woman to reckon with when Gloria caught Pat Nixon with her guard down. After the would-be First Lady finally agreed to an interview, she got a little bit overwhelmed and Steinem was able to turn out one of the most uniquely revealing statements by any aspiring First Lady in contemporary history. Pat Nixon had let herself go into something other than the traditional bland apple-pie garbage that has flowed in most First-Lady-candidate press conferences since Martha Washington began talking about life with George. "I've never had time to worry about who I admire or who I identify with," Mrs. Nixon said at the end of an outburst. "I've never had it easy, you know. I'm not like all of you . . . all those people who had it so easy." Gloria had traveled with the Nixon campaign, only as an observer. She had taken shots at Nixon personally but had never been able to puncture his political image as much as she did with the article on Mrs. Nixon.

In "Learning to Live with Nixon," she told about sparring for fifteen minutes with Mrs. Nixon and getting nothing but the dullest of answers until finally Pat said that the woman she most admired in history was Mamie Eisenhower. Gloria asked why.

"Because she meant so much to young people."

Gloria told Mrs. Nixon that Mamie didn't mean anything to young people, and Mrs. Nixon just folded up.

Mrs. Nixon then let go with beauties like "I never had time to dream about being anyone else. . . . I had to work . . . my parents died when I was a teen-ager, and I had to work my way through school. . . . I drove people all the way across country so that I could get back to New York and take training as an X-ray technician so I could work my way through college. . . . I worked in a bank while Dick was in the service. . . . Oh, I could have sat for those months like everyone else, but I worked in a bank and talked with people and learned all about their funny little customs. . . . I've never had

155

it easy. . . ." The only thing missing was Pat saying, "You'll never have Mrs. Nixon to kick around any more."

Both Nixons seem to have survived Gloria's gibes. Not every politician was as lucky. Richard Ottinger was a candidate for the United States Senate from New York when Gloria let go with her "Misgivings about Ottinger" as a lead article in the sophisticated *New York* Magazine. She attacked the Democrat with little more than the fact that he rubbed her intuitions wrong. Actually it was not so much her intuitions as it was a commitment to his opposition, Republican Charles Goodell, whom she liked especially because Vice President Spiro Agnew did not. Ottinger was defeated, and his Campaign Manager thinks it was because of Gloria Steinem. John Kenneth Galbraith, by then a strong Steinem buff, said, "When she cuts up people, the blood shows."

Gutsy Gloria has taken on some heavies before. She disagreed with Walter Cronkite, who was telling the country how great the moonshots were. She finally got around to saying what so many millions of Americans were thinking, and argued that we ought to solve our problems on the ground first before we worry about what is happening on the moon.

"Dear Gloria, until I saw you last night on television, I didn't know anyone could express exactly what I've been trying to say for years." This was a standard fan letter after one of her outspoken appearances.

It had been 1908 when Grandmother Steinem of Toledo, Ohio, was President of the Women's Suffrage Association and had gone as the United States delegate to the International Council of Women in Switzerland. She came back and testified before the United States Senate on suffrage. When she died in 1940, the *Toledo Blade* called her a remarkable woman who had helped shape the feminist movement in this country. She would be happier in that grave if she saw what Gloria was doing, keeping herself in good shape and reshaping the world.

Gloria Steinem has become maybe the most important filly in Kissinger's life—perhaps because he has been totally unsuccessful in getting her into the hay.

CHAPTER 16

✠

FALLEN ANGEL

Martin Gregory Stromberg and Helen Bertha Robertson were married on January 31, 1936, in St. George, Utah. He was nineteen and she was thirteen. Nearly seven years later they became the parents of a beautiful baby. Their little girl was born on Sunday, December 20, 1942, at the Albany Hospital in Albany, California. She weighed six pounds, fifteen ounces, and, according to the state records, was nineteen and a half inches long. That week Henry Kissinger was selling brushes in Manhattan trying to earn the money to pay for the first year's tuition at New York City College. Angel was too young for him just yet.

When Dr. Ralph Glass held her upside down and patted her fanny, he had no way of knowing that Angeline Bernice Stromberg would become Angel Tompkins and have her fanny patted twenty-eight years later by none other than Henry the K.

It is said that all living creatures are made in God's image, but even the most devout worshipers have not claimed that God ever looked as good as Angel Tompkins does today. Her mortal image was shaped by Chicago publicist Jim Feeley when he discovered that the young model could hold her own in a conversation and looked fantastic on a television screen.

Her youthful marriage to a Chicago biochemist had given her very little more than a commercial last name—Tompkins —and a son named Troy. But publicist Feeley went to work and, by the time his Angel was twenty-four, he had promoted Harry Nelson's multimillion-dollar Milway Catalog Company into a national promotional campaign featuring her. After using Angel to advertise everything from toasters to facial cream, Milway insured her pretty face for $1 million, and she was on her way.

Feeley was the right man to promote her. He had spent several years developing contacts in the television industry for the promotional tours he would arrange for everyone from Otto Preminger to "The Professor," author of the Angela Davis biography. A local public relations man who can occasionally deliver big-name guests for those low-rated daytime talk shows can usually fix an appearance for a newcomer as well.

Once the staff at Channel 26 (WCIU) got a look at Feeley's protégée, Angel had her own show. She was paired with Ted Weber, a young syndicated radio announcer, and was given one hour every Monday to rap about everything of interest to the housewives, invalids, and out-of-work citizens who stay glued to their idiot boxes in the morning. Feeley went overboard with a press build-up. He even induced a Chicago columnist to describe Kissinger's future playmate as having the "demeanor of a graceful Grecian goddess."

Angel's road to fame was winding but not altogether rocky. The Stromberg family relocated to Arizona when she was a kid, and she graduated from Phoenix High School. Her mother, who had married when she was not yet fourteen, died when Angel reached that same birthday. Her pretty face and body to match were noticed by more than the local high school heroes. She won her share of local and statewide beauty contests by turning on the local Chamber of Commerce officials and mixing her look of innocence with a southwestern Lolita manner.

To her credit, she turned down some minor opportunities with flaky Hollywood talent studios and decided to get an education first. She went to Texas Western College and got into modeling the way most pretty girls do—by dating a photographer. After a few minor successes in ads, she moved to the Midwest and enrolled at the University of Illinois, Champaign-Urbana. Among her studies were courses in the theater and the development of television technique on the University station. None of her teachers could offer any course in the technique of attracting the men who can do an ambitious girl a lot of good. This is an inborn instinct. Angel has it.

When she met Feeley, the young, highly successful public relations consultant ordered her to lose twelve pounds. She went on a Spartan diet, but it was worth it. Feeley had been right. When she incarnated weighing 116 pounds (she is five feet, seven inches tall), she had bone structure that would make a Greek statue jealous.

As in many another melodrama, her Pygmalion fell in love with her, and she went through the motions of falling in love with him. Feeley put up the money, the time, the energy, and the contacts to make her a success; and she looked beautiful. When she had milked the commercial market in Chicago, appeared in *Playboy*, and exhausted Feeley's bank account, she split for California, leaving little else but memories. Specifically, she took his furniture and personal belongings with her.

Her Chicago mentor had opened some Hollywood doors previously, and she plunged through. Within a short time she had done more than walk-on appearances in the *Wild, Wild West* and *Dragnet*. She then did her token All-American thing

161

by appearing in a Walt Disney disaster entitled *Hang Your Hat on the Wind*.

A casting director noticed Angel, and she landed a part opposite one of Hollywood's hottest actors, Elliott Gould, in *I Love My Wife*. Suddenly she was given the star treatment, and the absurd gossip columnists and movie magazine reporters started asking her about her "cucumber make-up secrets" and which "organic foods were most important." The blonde swinger actually told someone from the *Los Angeles Times* that the most important thing in life was "keeping pure." She warned that most foods were filled with nasty chemicals and said she drank only raw milk and used butter from certified cows.

At twenty-eight she was rediscovered. This time it was not by a talent scout or horny agent, but by an advance man for Kissinger whose hobby is finding sweet young things whom his boss will appreciate. For good reason, Kissinger kept the lid on his Angel Tompkins romance. He had already been badly burned by loud-mouthed Judy Brown. The embarrassment in diplomatic circles of having his picture on the front page of a scandal magazine with "a Hollywood starlet telling all" was still a touchy subject. But with discretion they dated and dated and dated!

Angel has always said that her mind was as good as her body. As a college-educated girl, she certainly was qualified to talk philosophically with the President's adviser. But, to her great chagrin, the President's adviser was not very much interested in her views on the country's economic problems, the social revolution, or aid to India. He had some problems of his own, and she seemed to provide a perfect solution.

CHAPTER 17

-------- ✠ --------

BARBARA HOWAR

"Henry, would that you could get in and out of Hollywood as quietly as you did Peking!"
— Barbara Howar

During the golden age of vaudeville, many animal at-tractions achieved greatness. One of those animal acts that flourished year after year was billed as Poffensberger's Bears. Unlike the competition, this troupe did not depend upon a great performer. Those run-of-the-mill acts made the rounds and died.

Poffensberger's greatness was his ability to keep changing bears without noticeably changing the performance. Some bears died, retired to zoos, or joined side shows. But Poffens-berger's rhythm never slackened, and the show always went on.

Reviewing Kissinger's adventures in rotating glamorous women reminds me of the master and his changing bears. Kissinger's "bears" may change too, but the act is always the same. It begins with a sudden appearance by the White House knight at a film festival, charity ball, or very exclusive private party. The press has been tipped that Kissinger will arrive at precisely 9:00 p.m. This is usually one hour after the latest of

163

the other guests are settled. It adds to the evening's excitement and Henry's reputation to let the suggestion bubble that he was delayed by a White House crisis.

Recently hosts have been inviting him to come late, hoping the air of mystery will precede him and turn on the other guests.

On Kissinger's arm is his latest bear. She is always beautiful, well-built, fabulously dressed, bejeweled, and generally recognizable even without him. The flash bulbs pop, and Kissinger fakes distress at the invasion of the privacy that he supposedly cherishes. But it was his own aides who had alerted the press to be there. Kissinger's only real social distress occurs when his presence escapes news coverage due to a slip-up by the host or the unexpected arrival of one of his few competitors for continuous media focus.

On very special occasions, a call from the White House will postpone the start of a major film or concert because Kissinger has been delayed on "crucial business." No less an affair than New York's world premiere showing of *The Godfather* was stayed for thirty minutes waiting for the Kissinger arrival.

Barbara Howar does not fit the image that the press has formed for regular Kissinger dates. She is in her mid-thirties, and dresses and talks well and even thinks. With a local TV interview show or as co-host of a nationally syndicated television talk show, she has matched gibes about the Nixon Administration with anyone who would give her a chance. Barbara Howar is an opinionated, gutsy girl, and she has been openly critical of the White House Cabinet members and their wives. For example, after a good many of Nixon's official family had settled in Watergate, a super-plush apartment complex on Virginia Avenue in Washington, D.C., Barbara described Watergate as "the ship of fools."

During the Administrations of John F. Kennedy and Lyndon B. Johnson, she was a prominent, swinging hostess whose parties were never dull. If necessary, she could always get herself up on a piano, show a bit of thigh, and dance the latest steps.

There was no reason why Barbara should not have grabbed the limelight from the other would-be Perle Mestas. After all, she had the two essential ingredients for any aspiring hostess—good contacts and a husband with a lot of money. Her spouse was a Washington contractor, a nice guy of Jordanian parentage. (She claimed that her parents expected her to arrive after the wedding on camelback.) The Howars had two children, Edmond and Bader (both of whom Kissinger professes to be very, very fond).

Through the swinging years, things went very well for the Howar family. Barbara would be the hostess responsible for a benefit or ball, where she would mix Washington's top politicos with intellectuals and show-business personalities just for the hell of it. Her husband took a more realistic view of her parties, which he claimed gave him a sharp, shooting pain in his pocket. But her contacts were good for his business.

Barbara was one of the leaders of the legions of Beautiful People who poured into President John F. Kennedy's Camelot for the purpose of lending class to the New Frontier. But she did not come into her own until 1964, when she was picked as one of the "Ladies for Lyndon." She surmises she was selected because the Johnson Administration was short on talent and long on desire. She ended up touring the United States on the Lady Bird Special—that ridiculous campaign train that traveled through eight southern states with buttons, banners, brochures, and bourbon. It was all dispensed to anyone who would take it. She sang the parody, "Hello, Lyndon," a hundred times a day and became pretty much of a late-night buddy for all the Birds, who appreciated her never-tiring sense

165

of humor and good looks. According to the *Ladies' Home Journal*, she even filled in as hairdresser for Lady Bird and Luci, though she did not possess the fine skills of Peggy Goldwater's personal hairtrician flown in from Goldwater's fashion house in Phoenix.

As a reward for her services to Lady Bird's plumage, Barbara was given the title of Coordinator of the Five Inaugural Balls. Lady Bird then delegated to her the sensitive and diplomatic task of purchasing the gowns for her daughters for daddy's inauguration. The girls were both away at boarding school; and Barbara was given an unlimited budget, a government limousine and driver, and public endorsement of her taste by the First Lady.

This gave Barbara a unique opportunity to be close to the Johnson family at home. Her recollections of some of the intimacies among those who were living in the White House are a riot. She remembers one dinner when the President was served a clear broth soup as a first course. "He never put his spoon in it, but turned to Mrs. Johnson and suggested that she keep her hot dishwater in the kitchen where it could be put to better use." Barbara's office and home became decorated with a wide variety of unsolicited autographed photos of LBJ and the family.

You cannot get an acidic sense of humor out of your system just because you're breathing the rarefied White House air, Barbara learned. One evening when the President was wearing a pair of casual pants that could only be described as baggy, he started teasing Barbara about why she did not quit tutoring his daughters and begin to give him fashion advice. She immediately replied that she would be glad to give him some free fashion advice concerning his pants. "When the seat wears out, upholster the porch couch with them." The President smiled a little.

At the Inaugural Ball, Johnson made a point of dancing with Barbara in front of the camera. She described her experience to members of the press as having been in "Hog Heaven."

The woman who would one day be rumored as Kissinger's best bet for his future wife was called upon to do a softening job on President Johnson to get him to accept his daughter Luci's suitor, Pat Nugent, whom he despised when he first met him. Finally, after several weeks of lobbying that would have made I.T.T.'s Mrs. Dita Beard jealous, the President grudgingly approved Luci's would-be hubby.

A frantic scramble developed over who was to do what and when and where for the wedding. Everybody got uptight with everybody, and Lady Bird compromised by splitting the responsibilities and the glory for the big White House social event. Barbara was given the opportunity of hostessing a very private dinner honoring Luci and Pat.

She quickly booked the roof gardens of one of Washington's top hotels and hired the rock band from Arthur's Club in New York, owned by Sybil Burton. There were to be so many cases of champagne and overstuffed vases of flowers, the decor would resemble something out of Louis XVI's opulent court. When Barbara submitted her proposed guest list to President Johnson, Henry Kissinger's name was not even on it. Although he possibly qualified intellectually, he was not yet close enough to LBJ, despite one little research project he had done for the current White House tenant. There were a great many Kennedy people on the list when it was submitted to the President for approval. There were none on the list when it was handed back. Although a strict press blackout was supposed to be in order, somebody leaked the details, and at least one television network had planned to have cameras set up with a helicopter to cover the event.

167

Hours before Barbara Howar had planned to go to the post office to mail the invitations to her private dinner party, honoring Luci and Pat, a phone call came from the White House. Press Secretary Liz Carpenter told Barbara that the affair was being canceled because Luci was "too exhausted." It took only one night and a few column notes for the word to get out all over Washington. The cancellation had nothing to do with Luci's exhaustion. Barbara Howar had been quickly and carefully deposed from White House good graces. She told reporters she did not know whether to cry or build a bomb shelter. The press got a little vicious. The woman who was once the confidante of the President's family was reduced in print to a "campaign road temporary hairdresser." All of those who had openly lobbied for Barbara's invitations now became openly rude.

The classic example of the LBJ vindictiveness came when her five-year-old daughter was told she had been replaced as a flower girl for Luci's wedding. At the last minute, when Barbara threatened a press conference over the insult to her daughter, Johnson capitulated. Top society reporters were bribed by White House spokesmen to follow the downgrading line on Barbara Howar. One syndicated reporter, Maxine Cheshire of the *Washington Post*, was offered a bridesmaidship if she would bring out a particular release which justified the White House banishment of Barbara.

When a member of the upper echelon of capital society falls from grace, very little attention is given to the reason. In the case of LBJ *et al.* versus Barbara Howar, it really did not matter. However much of a barbecue buff Johnson was, so long as he resided in the White House, he could order the deposal of anyone in town. Barbara's sin was pushing the strange Johnson sense of humor a little too far and getting involved in an intrafamily dispute once too often. It was easy to jump from that to being accused of taking advantage and abusing friendship with the First Family. In point of fact, Barbara Howar was no less or no more pushy then than she is today. She probably gave the Johnsons a lot more in the way of service and ideas than they gave her by way of prestige. No one has ever accused LBJ of being nice when it comes to people, and Washington, D.C., gets pretty rough when you take on a President, verbally or otherwise.

After the row with the temperamental Johnson-Bird family, high society dried up and shriveled away from Barbara Howar, avoiding her with a passion. One columnist described her as having fallen like a wilted flower from the last autumn. The crowning indignity came when she was dropped from Washington's Social Register, which means something—at least to those people who are in it. Barbara rather acidly commented it was like being asked to leave Klein's basement.

She did retain one important friend. One of the most fascinating old-timers in Washington, D.C., is Mrs. Alice Roosevelt Longworth, the elderly daughter of President Theodore Roosevelt. She reigned for half a century as one of the elite of Washington society. Even after the Johnson family froze up their friendship with Barbara, Mrs. Longworth kept a few important doors open to her friend.

In her pre-Kissinger-suitor days, when Barbara was nearly ostracized, she decided to reorganize her life. She got rid of a few pounds, a husband, and a big house, and started fresh. Her parties shifted from the top politicians to "real people" like Gloria Steinem—the reluctant heroine of Women's Liberation—who Kissinger swears is not his bedside companion.

Her post-divorce finances left her shaky, but she still had the value of the memories of days in the White House. She reduced them to a rather lengthy article in the *Ladies' Home Journal*. That great American literary institution has become the standard dispensation center for articles by former press secretaries, maids, cooks, butlers, gardeners, brothers, sisters, friends, and roommates of those in power. The article contained many shocking and astounding revelations. Certainly, the American people had a right to know that Lyndon Johnson mashed his peas with a spoon before eating them and that he fell asleep while watching home movies of his daughters (G rated, of course).

The exiled lady returned to the business of living her own life, but kept her finger in the charity ball business, despite the lack of assistance from LBJ's friends. She bounced back with a television show that got off with a good debut and looked like it might make it nationally.

Before Barbara Howar was linked with Henry Kissinger romantically, she had been described as a hard-headed New Woman. She could discuss homosexuality with Truman Capote and chat about the extracurricular sex life of public officials with Senator Barry Goldwater. She even managed to talk the television-shy Kissinger into appearing on her show.

It was quite a coup. The White House has been very hesitant to have Kissinger appear where his heavily accented voice can be heard. It is one thing to be kinky-haired, horn-rimmed, and Jewish. It is another to speak with a heavy German accent while discussing what the President of the United States is thinking. Nixon is always anxious to keep his midwestern All-American image intact.

Everyone at the television studio became an expert on the new Kissinger-Howar relationship after that show. A grip swears that the two of them were holding hands and carrying on like giddy teen-agers before and after in the make-up room, but Barbara's co-host claims that both were quite dignified at all times. In any event, Kissinger got his point across—he was interested. His message was received loud and clear by the swinging divorcee, who thought it might be a funny bit to get very friendly with the top aide to the President she publicly chewed up so often. Within days the telephone calls were being exchanged, together with those inexpensive but very personal gifts. From that beginning, it took very little to elevate Barbara to consort rank at some of the most glamorous functions in the country.

The columnists had a field day. They resurrected Barbara's political status by showing a cartoon of her sneaking back into the White House with Kissinger just as Johnson was going out the other door. With a broad smile she was able to say, "I came back . . ."

Barbara has developed a new power, which is based on the success of her television show, her natural wit, and her constant company-keeping with Super-Kraut. The *New York Times* dubbed her the leading eligible woman in Washington, D.C., society, and figured she was a natural to be linked with the leading bachelor in the capital city or anywhere else—Henry the K.

Talk comes easily to the talk-show hostess, and Barbara has been the source of secrets about Henry Kissinger's private life, both on her show and in newspaper interviews. She has talked about the décor in his Rock Creek townhouse, which she says is somewhat like a "midwestern Holiday Inn." She has described the furniture of the President's top adviser as "contemporary Grand Rapids hotel." She told friends that Kissinger's bedroom looked antiseptic; and the only room that seemed lived in was the library, which was loaded with books and political ornaments.

One secret she hasn't been able to let out is Kissinger's financial standing. His salary and expense account are not exactly public knowledge, but self-proclaimed experts figure that he is in the same bracket as a $50,000-a-year executive with a major corporation, and picking up a lot more fringes on the side. One can hardly imagine Henry coming in after his sneak visit to China and asking the President to go over his expenses with him. "I put the hotel in Pakistan on my Diner's Club card, but I forgot to keep the laundry receipts from China," somehow just doesn't ring true. At the same time, Henry's life style has not even begun to approach the palatial standards set by his millionaire brother. None of the Kissinger books has brought in much of a royalty. Public appearances do not pay honorariums to White House aides (or if they do, they are not accepted). Henry has kept his financial ledger quietly tucked away. He has, however, developed a reputation of being a little tight when it comes to tipping, according to employees in the hotels and restaurants he has frequented.

Of course, his position makes him a target for all sorts of sniping. One of the highest prices paid for political notoriety could be called the Pigeon Doctrine. It happens to top politicians, lawyers, actors, and even musicians. They are a mark for anybody with any sort of claim. Unreasonable bills are pressed by demanding creditors, and the mark is deprived of the right of contesting them for fear of the embarrassment of adverse publicity. At least one sweet young thing has tried to lead Kissinger on for more than publicity support. She got nowhere. Henry did not develop the tough skin necessary for world politics by being a marshmallow in his personal life. The girl is still in Paris, and her relationship with Kissinger, or lack of it, has enhanced neither her career nor her pocketbook.

Kissinger carries the highest security clearance and is the only person aside from Nixon privileged to view those documents marked "For the President's Eyes Only." It was this high degree of confidence and power that produced the facetious but frightening slogan I mentioned earlier: "If anything should happen to Kissinger . . . then Nixon would be President."

Fortunately, Barbara Howar does not need a top security clearance. As a television personality, her business is disseminating information.

When someone criticized Barbara's readiness to talk, she observed, "There is an immense secrecy in this town, and it's such a thumping bore. I don't want to be privy to atomic secrets, but in the political area everyone plays his cards so close to his chest you can't tell if it's a man or a woman."

Her best quip was the public lament: "Henry, would that you could get in and out of Hollywood as quietly as you did Peking!" She does hasten to defend Kissinger's taste in women, especially starlets, by observing, "After all, if you're with Golda Meir all day, you don't need Mrs. Gandhi all night. You want Jill St. John!"

Finally, she has attempted to put the more outlandish gossip about Kissinger to rest by insisting that, "Henry doesn't have the time to be a real swinger." He does, however, have the time to be seen with Barbara frequently at Washington nightspots, parties, the theater, and concerts.

What do they see in each other? First of all, Barbara says, "I like to see class in anyone—a certain amount of professionalism, a certainty tempered by a little kindness. Show me a good old strumpet who does it with class, and I'll take my hat off to her." Kissinger does have his own special kind of class— at least, he has consistency in most things he does.

Again, she has said, "I have no use for uncommitted people." Kissinger is not merely committed, he is at the very center of power in this country and the world. Like others, she says Henry is one of the few colorful people left in Washington. He knows how to pay attention to her, is willing to talk

173

intelligently with her, and is a social and political entrée to everything everywhere.

On Henry's side the motivations are a bit more obvious. Barbara is beautiful, bright, and available. Besides, she likes him.

One would think her politics would be something of a liability. She makes no secret of being a "left-liberal Democrat." She has made the Nixon Administration the butt of some pretty harsh jokes. Also, she has a pronounced sympathy for the Women's Liberation Movement. This seems to indicate a certain perverseness Henry demonstrates in choosing women. Either they have no brains at all, or if they do they are antagonistic to Kissinger's boss.

On the other side of the ledger, Barbara Howar is a polished and attractive woman—one he can take out in public without any fear of scandal or of Barbara's making some incredible gaffe in front of reporters. She is a humorous defender—and that comes in handy. She can also serve as an excellent source for reporters, serving to allay particularly bad rumors. More important, she offsets the starlet-stud image he had acquired.

Barbara Howar is older than most of Henry's girls, and she wears an air of attractive maturity. She is the perfect product of Washington society and, when Henry wants that kind of image, she is ideal for supplying it.

Henry's women—at least, the ones he is willing to be seen with—have very different images, and each can serve to enhance or modify the social charisma of Super-Kraut in some way. Henry seems to alternate among them, and their images, as if he were constantly trying on and taking off a number of expensive coats.

The Secret Swinger and the Washington Hostess—even if they had not been seeing each other—would have been thrown together through gossip because the idea is so perfect. By background, by connections, by experience, intelligence, and temperament, Barbara Howar is ideally suited to be a front-runner for the coveted Mrs. Kissingership.

CHAPTER 18

———————— ✠ ————————

HENRY'S STARS

It is believed that during anyone's political season no fewer than several hundred hustling men survive in our nation's capital dead broke. Yet, they live in style. The game is always to have a party to go to. If you just follow the diplomatic tour, you can avoid buying meals for nine months and twenty days. (Everybody—even freeloaders—goes away for the summer.)

Start to assimilate this life style by realizing that over a hundred foreign nations maintain Embassies in Washington, D.C. They vary in plushness from the distinctive French Ambassador's residence, with tennis courts and transplanted Parisian gardens, to the barren home of the Republic of Dahomey, where Ambassador DeSouza emphasizes his nation's plight by living beneath the standards for decadent splendor his colleagues prefer.

Each Embassy exists for three very precise purposes. First, it must insure that its home nation keeps hold of whatever American foreign aid it is receiving. Second, it must find more American foreign aid to receive. And finally, it must make sure that Chad, Bhutan, Senegal, and the big guys do not get more than their fair share.

Regardless of the degree of international sophistication

they have acquired, foreign diplomats cannot understand American political life. "If he has no troops, why is he the Postmaster-General?" they ask. In the absence of a decipherable chart of the game plan for getting things done in the United States government (many natives of our land would like one, too), the usual diplomatic course is to try to touch all bases—even if some of them seem to be out in left field.

Accordingly, it is the principal responsibility of the aides and attachés that insulate foreign Ambassadors to secure as guests for their Embassy functions a wide variety of influential officials. They also seek new friends for their government from every government office that has a budget or a voice. The policy is: When in doubt, always be gracious! Many more powerless flunkies have sipped brandy and gobbled caviar on Embassy Row than Cabinet members.

Traditionally, each member of the Senate and the House of Representatives, as well as major department heads, is invited to diplomatic soirees. It takes only a secretarial contact for a presentable extra man to snare an invitation. Each Embassy is good for a party on the birthday of its founding father or on the anniversary of its independence or most recent revolution. Most will find an excuse to honor a favorite son at another time of the year so as to get all the VIP's it missed the first time around. The bigger nations will be good for some type of party every few months. The social whirl averages out to 2.9 potential free meals per Embassy in any one year, or 290 ways to avoid buying dinner. Since it is gauche for Embassies to compete on the same night, most of the political year is covered.

Each year one high-ranking official is considered the prize social catch. The Embassies compete with the lobbyists, and they in turn compete with the local society leaders. A newly appointed Supreme Court Justice is a major coup unless he is overexposed, like Chief Justice Warren E. Burger, or a dud, like William H. Rehnquist. When Nixon crossed party lines and brought former Texas Governor John B. Connally, Jr., to the Cabinet as Secretary of the Treasury, he became temporary first choice of those wanting their parties to reach the newspaper columns. His stature as a social lion lasted about a month.

The game goes on, with each party-giver outdoing his or her neighbor in décor, contemporary musicians, and asinine portions of every food imaginable, usually served by an armada from Abbey-Rent-A-Waiter. Limousines are rented and fur coats are rented and, if things get tough, guests are rented. One publicist makes a good living booking Senators, movie stars, and a Duke and Duchess for $500 per head per evening up. If there was an international meeting of taxpayers, the six thousand members of the Washington, D.C., diplomatic corps would be out of work overnight.

It is expected that every hostess season her group-salad with a token intellectual and/or radical. The invisible guidebooks give preference to Harvard types who project a professorial image, look a little awkward, and are tastelessly dressed. They can be counted on to get into a loud argument toward the end of the evening, offending a conservative and making the occasion memorable for all.

Two cyclones hit the District of Columbia social scene with the inauguration of Richard Milhous Nixon in 1969. One was a preoccupation with astrology. The other was Henry M. Kissinger. Reading the stars became a regular ritual, and those who had memorized the morning horoscope were guaranteed an opening in any conversation.

Kissinger was a blessing. First, he looked like a professor, with the high forehead and intelligent gaze of a smirking superior. Second, he was a perfect minority representative—a Jew

179

who did not flaunt it. Then there was an added bonus: his preoccupation with bosomy broads of the show-business cult who substituted cleavage for cleverness whenever they accompanied him.

In an age when job applicants are sometimes asked their birth signs by astrology-conscious corporate executives, anything is possible. Those who believe in the daily prognosis of the stars are fervent worshipers and pay all sorts of tribute to their astrologers. Sometimes their faith seems vindicated. Once in a while a classic case appears, to the delight of the sign readers and their followers—as well as book publishers. To that end Henry Kissinger is the all-time, all-trait-bearing, most Geminian Gemini ever to admit where the sun was on the day he was born.

Kissinger is in good company as a Gemini. His sign-mates include diverse notables such as the late President John F. Kennedy, Che Guevara, Constantine II, . . . and me. When the printers of those little cards that cost a penny when you get your wrong weight wrote out the Gemini traits, they pegged Kissinger right down to his moon risings. The basic attribute of those with the sign of the twins is two personalities in one person who can change his mind as readily as he changes shirts, jobs, or women.

The prototype Gemini's intellectual qualities correspond to many of Kissinger's more obvious attributes. According to one principal horoscope dispenser: "Kissinger is a textbook classic. He possesses the really important Gemini traits—he reads quickly, talks quickly, and even listens fast. He is full of nervous energy and loves to match wits with people of equal brain power." (He will not admit to superior brain power in anyone.) Geminis are most impatient with indecisive people. That may account for Kissinger's closeness to President Nixon, who makes decisions quickly, whether right or wrong.

It appears, if you consult all of the prescribed qualities of all of the birth signs, that Geminis should have the most consistently brilliant sense of humor, tact, diplomacy, and gregarious mental energy.

Supposedly, we June birthday babies are unpredictable in love, naturally fickle, and always hungry for new friends. At least nine California-based "actresses" will attest to Henry's qualifications as a dedicated Gemini in that regard. Most Geminis marry more than once and live a split life with two homes, two cars, two pets, two interests, and two often very different life styles.

Again, the astrologers must have known Henry was coming when they published a 1924 astrology chart listing Geminis as "not handsome, but strangely attractive to women."

Kissinger even conforms to the Gemini physical requirements—a long, sharp nose, a receding hairline (from a lot of brain activity), and the energy to be constantly on the move.

Sex for political gain is a way of life in any nation's capital. Washington, D.C., far from being an exception, is the pacesetter in bedroom diplomacy. No lobbyist, contractor, or visiting ambassador is worth his salt without at least one loyal pro or well-trained amateur who can pry out information à la Mata Hari while doing her thing.

Naturally, a Presidential adviser is a prime target.

One ambitious African delegation kept sending a magnificent mulatto named Monique to Washington functions that Kissinger was expected to attend. The new independent African nation felt the White House was not paying enough attention to their problems, and Monique could help the President's right-hand man see the light. One comment by Kissinger at a National Security Council meeting could open the door to American loans, surplus food shipments, and a boost in stature at the United Nations.

The girl was French and North African. Mostly she was beautiful. She was dressed and jeweled to meet what the emerging nation's delegation judged to be the Kissinger taste. Then a jealous delegate from another African consulate learned about the plot and tipped off a Kissinger security aide. An embarrassing international incident was avoided when Kissinger's would-be seducer was hustled out of the country because of a minor passport violation.

At a typical cocktail party you can find a usual assortment of well-groomed, high-ranking government officials trying to evade their wives. It is time to try to set up another matinée with a willing secretary. A half dozen Capitol Hill hotels do more business with daytrippers than regular guests.

Across the room among the beautiful people at such a party may appear a nondescript middle-aged little guy with thick glasses and hair to match. He is deeply involved in conversation with the most ravishing beauty in the room. You wonder: How can this be?

The house rules permit comparing notes on other guests. Later over hors d'oeuvres you nail the pretty lady and ask, "Why Kissinger?" She reports, "He's very interesting. . . . He's got a great line. He starts witty and gets brilliant. After a while he gets down to business."

The Kissinger approach is cute. He tells his target: "I'm just an immigrant Harvard Professor." Now he has her going, and it is time for the knockout punch. Get this! "Yet, I find myself in this beautiful home with these beautiful people talking to a most beautiful girl. I know it's not me . . . it's the White House. If I wasn't the President's closest adviser, I wouldn't be here. . . . I'd be just another Professor dining in a lonely room."

The White House had adopted a hands-off policy on Kissinger's after-hours activities. But a well-meaning protocol aide at the State Department took it upon himself to suggest to his counterpart in Kissinger's office that Henry would be better off with a higher-class date at certain diplomatic affairs. Kissinger took the hint, and after that his two special-occasion "legitimate ladies" were imported as needed.

The first was Nancy Maginnes, a regular Kissinger companion in New York whom he met in his Rockefeller days. Nancy was a research assistant for the New York Governor, assigned to dig up helpful tidbits for Kissinger and Company as they tried to steal delegates for Rocky at the 1968 GOP Convention in Miami Beach.

Kissinger was out of his element. The delegates he was pitching were professional politicians, not academicians. Nonetheless, "I enjoyed it," Henry recalls. But he insisted he had no deep interest in campaigning. "It's one thing to do that for three days; it would be another thing to have to spend your life that way."

Nancy was always there at those late post-mortem sessions when Rockefeller's staff would mourn the loss of promised votes and try to hype each other for the next day's battle. When it was over, Nancy was still there. She was a perfect companion for the egotistical Kissinger. She would never compete. When they arrived at a party or a premiere, she would slip into the background looking tall and silent while Henry took the spotlight.

Sometimes her unobtrusiveness backfired. At the New York opening of *The Godfather*, Henry and Nancy arrived late and, as the photographers began snapping pictures, Nancy disappeared into the crowd. Kissinger gave a brief warm greeting to actress Ali McGraw, and the photographers went wild. As a result, several major newspapers carried the story of a

183

McGraw-Kissinger romance. Their "proof": the pictures of Henry and Ali, from which they assumed he had escorted her to the premiere.

Kissinger-watching and second-guessing are favorite sports for several gossip columnists. At least one of the watchful witches predicts Henry will marry Nancy. After all, "It only makes sense for her to be in the background if she is the one he is really serious about." Also, there is a total information black-out on her at the Rockefeller office.

Miss Maginnes is the tallest of Henry's ladies, with a two-inch advantage over her sometimes escort. She dresses conservatively, and has a constant political smile. She also doubles as Henry's personal link with his former boss, Nelson Rockefeller.

The second mystery woman who appears when the wholesome look is needed is a lower-echelon CBS news producer, Margaret Osmer. She pops up in a gown from which she pops out at a major share of Kissinger's cultural appearances.

Osmer is a hybrid. She looks as glamorous as Henry's West Coast contingent, but is known to also have a brain. She was on Kissinger's arm at the social event of the year when the Kennedy Center for the Performing Arts in Washington opened with the production of Leonard Bernstein's *Mass*.

Margaret's reputation peaked when she showed up as Kissinger's "cover" at a Parisian restaurant when he was on his secret mission to end the Vietnam War. She never knew what was going on.

Kissinger enjoys dating the women he meets in his work. Margaret was assigned to do his biography for the Mike Wallace show, *Sixty Minutes*. Of fifty-six network news correspondents, she was then the only female. A date followed and, after Kissinger spent one evening with his deeply tanned and well-endowed new fan, she was hooked.

Beyond their social rapport, there were mutual on-the-job advantages for Margaret and Henry. After all, the White House had been having fits over CBS news policy, and she would be a pipeline. While the White House press secretaries were jubilating, CBS was not sleeping. Word reportedly went down from the very top that, although the network does not "mix" in reporters' personal lives, the Osmer-Kissinger relationship should be encouraged. Perhaps there would be an exclusive they could beat the competition to. Suddenly Margaret's bosses became very liberal whenever she wanted time off. If those interested observers in high places could have their way, Henry and Margaret would never be star-crossed lovers.

A good many forces besides the stars clearly would like to rule Henry's life. Although some of his social predilections may have been predestined by the heavens, he seems to have a lot of help from ambitious Washington hostesses, emerging nations, Embassy protocol experts, and network executives. Whether he owes it to the stars or something else, Henry Kissinger obviously is enjoying all of the advantages of his rich, full social life.

———————— ✠ ————————

CHAPTER 19

THE ANDERSON TIPS

Jack Anderson is a self-confessed muckraker. In seven hundred newspapers each day, his column, "The Washington Merry-Go-Round," reaches more Americans and visitors of every age than his competition wants to admit. Anderson says he likes to write for milkmen. Lately his market has increased, as young America has made a kind of Ralph Nader hero of the former protégé of the late Drew Pearson.

Anderson believes that there are Congressmen cheating on their income tax, fooling around at government expense, handling official government business while drunk, and the public has a right to know about it—so they can stop it. He believes there are White House officials who are perennial liars and who cover up their personal peccadilloes by claiming Presidential immunity. He attacks the Military Establishment for its inefficiency and for operating the Pentagon as the personal country club for a "handful of top Generals and civilian advisers." In an evangelistic tone, he trumpets on college campuses, "The incestuous relationship between government and big business thrives in the dark. . . . When those responsible for it get caught in the sunlight, they are like fish out of water. They flip and they flop. They backfire."

For some years before the late Drew Pearson's death in

1969, Anderson and Pearson co-authored "The Washington Merry-Go-Round." Pearson was a Quaker who earned a reputation as one of the world's most relentless and usually most accurate political scandalmongers. Anderson is also devout, but a Mormon (a former Mormon missionary), and the father of nine. Since inheriting the Pearson mantle, his implacable investigative reporting has plummeted at least half a dozen national figures to their ruin. And, the columnist admitted to me, his exposés probably had something to do with a couple of suicides.

Since 1969, Anderson has emerged from Pearson's shadow as a powerhouse to be feared by White House and Capitol Hill tenants. His name is as familiar to television audiences as that of Henry Kissinger. One Washington colleague commented: "Jack has had more stories in the *New York Times* than any *New York Times* reporter." Since Pearson's death, Jack has increased his column's circulation by some 130 newspapers. His publishers estimate that about 150 million people read Jack Anderson, and that surely makes him one of the most potent forces in the United States.

Anderson has an idealistic concept of American government. He believes the Constitution is "divinely inspired." And he interprets it as forbidding any type of government secrecy that allows anyone in public office to mislead the public. "The framers of the Constitution did not intend that," he maintains. He shares consumer advocate Ralph Nader's preoccupation with the influence of private power in spending public money. The columnist is most at home when exposing some corrupt deal involving multimillion-dollar government contracts.

Even before his hard-hitting columns on the International Telephone and Telegraph Company and some high government officials early in 1972 (his disclosures resulted in a full-scale Congressional investigation), Anderson had an impressive track record. In 1966, when Drew Pearson was still alive, Anderson took on Senator Thomas Dodd and exposed the Connecticut Democrat's misuse of campaign funds. The Senator was censured by his colleagues and defeated by the voters.

Then Anderson set his sights on Nixon's friend, California Senator George Murphy, who the columnist claimed had remained on the Technicolor, Inc., payroll while serving in the Senate. In 1970 Murphy was defeated by the youthful Democrat John V. Tunney.

Anderson published a story in 1970 about the Washington influence-peddling scandal involving Nathan Voloshen and Martin Sweig, who had used House of Representatives Speaker John McCormack's office in connection with some illegal lobbying activities. Sweig was convicted of perjury. Voloshen pleaded guilty to charges brought against him. McCormack decided to retire from politics.

More recently, Anderson took on a Congressman from Pennsylvania, J. Irving Whalley, and accused him of taking kickbacks and padding his payroll. Whalley suddenly announced he would not seek reelection.

Anderson's investigative zeal is not limited to those who reside on Capitol Hill. In the course of his muckraking activities, he implicated a couple of Latin American officials in an involved international narcotics scheme.

When a muckraker falls on his face, the whole country knows about it. The biggest goof in Anderson's catalog was Chappaquiddick. After Mary Jo Kopechne drowned in a car accident on Chappaquiddick Island involving Senator Edward M. Kennedy, he made the mistake of printing an unconfirmed story that both John and Edward Kennedy had often visited the island. In fact, JFK had never been there, and July 18, 1969, the day of the fatal accident, was the first time Edward Kennedy had been there. It was a rare boner for the crusading columnist (his apology to Senator Thomas Eagleton in the summer of 1972 not withstanding).

Anderson has put together a network of contacts in key government offices that may rival the Central Intelligence Agency's roster. He doesn't bother to question the motive of someone who gives him a lead on a top story. "If an individual is out to get his boss, that's his business," Anderson says. But he does check his sources carefully and, as a result, more essential information finds its way to the American people through an Anderson column than is usually found in a whole handful of government press releases.

It was Anderson who took on Kissinger and the White House and forced the Administration once again into a secret document controversy while it was still reeling from the battle over the Pentagon Papers. It was Anderson who somehow secured secret records from the National Security Council. It would have been useless for anyone to call them forgeries—it was too obvious that they were authentic. The disclosures involved the Nixinger Administration's attitude toward Pakistan and India and Bangla Desh—a credibility gap between its internal secret documents and its public statements.

Early in 1971 hostilities had erupted between East and West Pakistan. A by-product of the partitioning of India in 1947, Pakistan was a curious nation, with East and West Pakistan separated by nearly a thousand miles of Indian territory and a vast economic and language gulf. A civil war erupted over issues of autonomy, and millions of refugees fled from East Pakistan into India.

East Pakistan declared its independence under the name, Bangla Desh. West Pakistan claimed that India was equipping and training the rebel forces and was really behind the whole military action in Bangla Desh. In 1971 over seven million people fleeing from the military suppression of the autonomy movement in East Pakistan poured into India. The enormous refugee burden put India's economy in crisis, and thousands died of cholera and exposure. Indian troops and tanks moved toward the East Pakistan border. By fall there would be a widening Asian war to deal with, as India and Pakistan met in battle.

On July 6, 1971, Presidential Aide Kissinger arrived in New Delhi for a visit with Prime Minister Indira Gandhi. American military aid to Pakistan had been a sore point with the Indians for some time, and demonstrators greeted Kissinger with signs protesting it. "Kissinger of death, go back," was chanted.

Kissinger's visit apparently did not heal the wounds.

In August, 1971, India signed a twenty-year friendship treaty with the Soviet Union.

At the United Nations, as year-end drew near, Ambassador George Bush followed the Nixon line and placed the blame for the war on India and demanded a cease-fire and withdrawal of all troops behind their own borders.

Late in December, 1971, Jack Anderson dropped his bombshell. He had secured secret records from the National Security Council. The documents were detailed reports of conferences headed up by Henry Kissinger when the Administration was trying to determine how to deal with the India-Pakistan crisis. The reports showed that Kissinger had told others in the conference that President Nixon was "giving him hell" because fellow government officials were not following the White House lead and taking the side of Pakistan, as he had instructed. The documents revealed that Kissinger was definitely espousing an anti-Indian policy during his briefing of other government officials. He said he had been instructed by President Nixon to criticize the Indian aggression and he did so repeatedly.

191

Anderson had the documents—had held them for some time, he says—but did not decide to publish them until Kissinger held a remarkable background briefing for Washington newsmen. After one question from the press, Kissinger said, "First of all, let us get a number of things straight. There have been some comments that the Nixon Administration is anti-Indian. This is totally inaccurate."

That statement was an outright lie, Anderson contended, and in the dispute that followed in the next few weeks, it was Anderson's game, set, and match all the way over Kissinger.

Anderson conceded that President Nixon and Professor Kissinger might be within their rights in being critical of India for taking an aggressive policy. What was wrong was secretly advising government officials to speak out with one view and then denying it to the press and the American people. That kind of behavior violated the Anderson code, and Jack Anderson blew the whistle on Henry Kissinger.

Confusion was compounded when Kissinger gave Senators an off-the-record report, and Senator Barry Goldwater told the *New York Times* about that briefing. It seems that Henry had not made perfectly clear his desire for anonymity. Then it was learned that Moscow had poured more than a billion dollars' worth of military aid into India over the past few years.

There were swift repercussions from the Anderson tips.

Senator Edmund S. Muskie (then a leading Presidential contender) and other Democrats quickly realized the political value of the leaked documents, and used the Anderson revelations to attack the Administration's handling of the India-Pakistan crisis. They pointed out the plight of the Bangla Desh in the light of Pakistani atrocities, and painted the Nixinger Administration as cold and ruthless.

Anderson says he was threatened with prosecution unless he told where he got the documents. He refused. The FBI began to investigate. They narrowed the list of "suspects" to some two hundred government officials who might have taken the papers from the National Security Council and given them to Jack Anderson. Security officers were shaken: If comments by the President's top adviser on the delicate subject of the India-Pakistan dispute could be removed so easily, then might not more secret government papers be lifted?

The war slowly quieted down, and the American public again focused on Vietnam's daily statistics. The most significant U.S. casualty in the Bangla Desh fighting had been the Administration's credibility and integrity. The messenger who brought the bad news of those casualties to the American people was a renegade reporter named Anderson.

Jack Anderson was not prosecuted. He did win a Pulitzer Prize for his reporting of the affair. The significance of the award, Anderson noted, was that it "was given for exposing Government secrets." He deduced that the Pulitzer board by their action had recognized "the right of the people to know what goes on in the backrooms of government. . . ."

That was Jack Anderson's credo right down the line. It would haunt the Nixinger Administration for quite a while.

CHAPTER 20

—————— ✠ ——————

THE FIRST TERM

Mothers of small boys in this country no longer talk in terms of their babies growing up to be President. The desire to have the child prodigy reach the White House has become as tarnished as many other American dreams of success.

More likely now you can hear mothers and sons agreeing that no man is fit to be President . . . and, if he takes the job, he is crazy. The complex day-to-day decisions make it impossible to please everybody all of the time and even make it difficult to please anybody any of the time. The strain has shown on every White House tenant in contemporary times.

It took less than genius to realize that, when Richard Milhous Nixon became President of the United States on January 20, 1969, it would be one of the most difficult terms that any American Chief Executive had ever faced. The tasks that confronted the President-elect were enormous. He had promised to withdraw half a million American troops from Vietnam. Inflation was soaring to a danger point, and the country's foreign trade was languishing.

There was crime in the streets. From every corner of the nation, urban officials were desperately pleading for money to save their decaying cities. The infusion of federal funds into a variety of municipal plans brought criticism from rural areas who felt they were not getting their shake. The welfare rolls had swelled to the point where the cost of just administering the give-away of money ran into millions each year. Racial de-segregation of the schools was still a pipe dream and had to be completed quickly to lower the seething racial tensions in the country. The Blacks and the Browns and the poor and the young, and finally the women, were in open revolt.

If the people could somehow survive their own conflicts, there was always the problem of the environment, which had deteriorated to a point where children were being kept home from school in some major cities because of pollution alerts. The battle lines had been drawn between big industry and consumer action groups on environmental issues.

Internationally, the Soviet Union was moving full steam ahead in its arms race with the United States. Experts no longer talked in terms of American superiority. India, Paki-stan, Japan, Israel, Laos, and a dozen other nations presented pressing problems for the President and Kissinger and their team when they took over in 1969.

No one thought of Nixon as a miracle worker. It is hard to imagine a miracle worker of the stature to solve the problems the Nixinger Administration faced. President Kennedy's New Frontier or LBJ's Great Society or even FDR's New Deal could not have handled the full load of pressures that existed in 1969.

The politics of the new Administration seemed at first merely to be a public relations campaign to minimize blunders, maximize achievements, and try to get reelected in 1972.

Aside from Kissinger, Nixon's personnel selections were not outstanding. Kissinger headed up the staff of relatively competent men who were low on academic achievement, out-side of Henry, but had plenty of good political savvy.

The biggest problem that Nixon inherited that would

jeopardize his reelection prospects was the Vietnam War and the problem of getting GI's home. Nixon could not quickly retreat from his position of tough-mindedness with respect to America's obligations under treaties and moral policy. At the same time, there was his promise to get American troops out; and, if he did not, there was a good chance he would not be re-elected President. Nixon had originally favored U.S. intervention in Vietnam; and he did not make a move until the American people became tremendously vocal and obviously dedicated to ending the war. Finally, the new Administration accepted the inevitability of pulling out completely as the pressure of public opinion mounted. Nixon had to capitulate. The White House came out with a troop withdrawal plan, designed by Kissinger and approved by the Pentagon, to reduce American forces to 184,000 by December of 1971.

The new household word became "Vietnamization." The arming of South Vietnam forces to the point where they could keep up the war against the enemy became a compelling goal. At the same time, Kissinger quarterbacked a move for negotiated settlements that would not lose America too much face. He urged Nixon to propose optional plans, including a mutual withdrawal of forces, new Vietnam elections, release of prisoners of war, U.N. or some other international supervision of the peace, and an immediate ceasefire in place. The stubborn North Vietnamese and the cocky Vietcong would accept one, four, or five, but never "all of the above."

No one knew then of Kissinger's secret talks. There had been a token pullout, but it was nothing near what was needed or promised by Nixon in his campaign rhetoric. Pickets against the war surrounded the White House and appeared on campuses and in front of government offices in major cities.

In late 1969, the Vietnam moratorium demand drew a monumental number of men, women, and children from every walk of life to the nation's capital. The President took to television, attempting to overcome the antiwar movement by hunting for "the great silent majority." His plea did little substantively, but it had a dramatic political effect. For a while the Nixinger team could coast while the nation divided itself into silent majority, vocal minority, and their cyclic counterparts. Or so it seemed.

On April 30, 1970, Nixon dropped a bomb—and he did not use aircraft to deliver it—it came on TV. ". . . This is the decision I have made: In cooperation with the armed forces of South Vietnam, attacks are being launched this week to clean out major sanctuaries on the Cambodian-Vietnam border. . . . Tonight American and South Vietnam units will attack the headquarters for the entire Communist military operation in South Vietnam."

The purpose was supposedly to smash the hideouts of the enemy and to cut off supplies that were the constant threat to the Vietnamization program. U.S. troop withdrawals were being held up, according to Nixon's military advisers, because of the constant flow of reinforcements and supplies from Cambodia. It was all perfectly proper to the military; and it was equally as improper to the rest of the country.

The apocalyptic rhetoric used by Nixon and Kissinger in justifying American forces in Cambodia wiped out any progress that had been made in quieting the campuses. All hell broke loose around the country, and there was a reawakening of the antiwar movement that must have made former President Johnson gloat. Even some Republicans prepared to challenge Nixon at the polls. The President blew his cool and, while talking at the Pentagon, said in front of a group of reporters that the demonstrators were "bums."

Within three days at Kent State University in northeastern Ohio, the National Guard was called out and fired on students protesting the new Cambodia invasion. Eleven young men and women were wounded, and four were killed. The slaughter of students provided fuel for anti-American newspapers around the world. Glaring headlines of internal revolution in the United States keynoted a massive international propaganda campaign. The bloodshed shook the country. As campus after campus blew up, school after school closed down. Nixon's political stature was at its lowest ebb, except with the far right-wing hardliners who did not care about a little bloodshed from the "bums" in college. Kissinger advised Nixon to ease off the military operation. The President listened, and finally the demonstrators quieted.

The nation went through a cooling-off period. The troop level and casualties dropped in Vietnam. The war issue began to slide, and America became preoccupied once again with the violence in Chicago, Detroit, Miami, and Washington, D.C. It was almost as if we could take the war for granted as a syndicated adventure series, with the latest chapter being narrated by Walter Cronkite each evening.

By this time, Americans were beginning to realize that Professor Henry Kissinger of Harvard was not the ordinary Presidential adviser. Somehow he had developed an intimate rapport with the Chief Executive and acquired responsibilities beyond anyone else in the government.

The news media became curious about Henry's private life. A story about his latest date would appear next to a Presidential announcement quoting Kissinger's findings on a particular problem with the Russians or Chinese. Kissinger's itinerary began looking like something out of Walter Mitty. In one evening he would be swashbuckling at a Hollywood party with sexy movie stars and the jet set. Later that night he would leave by Air Force jet for a critical meeting with the representatives of North Vietnam. Henry began working and living even more frantically. Kissingerisms began to catch on, and the idea of Dr. Strangelove come-to-life with a sense of humor and taste in broads almost made it easier to accept the world's crises.

And then in February, 1971, ten months after Nixon's invasion of Cambodia, the nation calmly turned on their TV sets to learn that the White House had approved the invasion of Laos by South Vietnamese troops supported by American air power and "advisers."

The United States went on about its business. A poster appeared that week in a San Francisco shop: "JOIN THE ARMY, TRAVEL TO UNUSUAL PLACES, MEET INTERESTING PEOPLE, AND KILL THEM."

Aside from Vietnam, there were other problems for the Nixon Administration to overcome—some of its own creation.

One of the few areas of Presidential decision-making that Kissinger stayed out of was the donnybrook over Nixon's determination to pack the Supreme Court. From the beginning, the President had made it clear that he considered the right to appoint justices to the Supreme Court the right to appoint exclusively men who shared his political philosophy and would help judicially to enforce his campaign promises. Chief Justice Warren Burger, whom Nixon appointed in 1969, publicly shared Nixon's "law and order" views and felt that the Warren Court had gone too far on Constitutional guarantees in criminal cases. The abortive attempt to appoint two other men who would share his political philosophy and fulfill campaign obligations to Senator Strom Thurmond of South Carolina, and other Southerners, was a stunning defeat. When he nominated Southerners Clement Haynsworth and G. Harrold Carswell to the Supreme Court, he suffered the catastrophe of Senate rejection. It was the first time in history that a President's two successive Supreme Court appointments had met such a fate.

The Supreme Court appointments precipitated a long and bitter fight. After the Haynsworth nomination was rejected, Nixon proposed Carswell. When Attorney General John N. Mitchell reviewed Harrold Carswell's record and said, "He's almost too good to be true," he displayed value judgments the Senate didn't share. His words were among the opening guns of a seventy-eight-day political war which proved Carswell was the wrong man in the wrong place at the wrong time.

The NAACP took a position against the nomination on the ground that it was "clearly designed to compromise the Negroes' future judicial protection far beyond the life of any single Administration," and the *New York Times* ran an editorial calling the nomination "a shock" and adding that it "almost suggests an intention to reduce the significance of the Court by lowering the caliber of its membership."

One leading Republican Senator, who had cast a crucial vote against Carswell, called the choice an attempt to rub the Senate's nose in the mess it had made of the Haynsworth nomination. The Justice Department had rated Carswell considerably below Haynsworth and a few other candidates.

After the protracted fight over Haynsworth and Carswell, Nixon proclaimed that the country would never accept a southern judge (no matter how qualified he was), and he reached out for his new Chief Justice's best friend, Harry Andrew Blackmun of Minnesota.

Alert newsmen discovered that Blackmun had been best man at Warren Burger's wedding. Yet, despite fifty years of intimate friendship, when Blackmun was asked on April 15, 1970, by a *New York Times* reporter if his friendship with Burger had anything to do with the nomination, he replied, "I

201

wouldn't know anything about that." Responding to a similar question as to whether sharing Nixon's views had anything to do with his appointment, he said, "I wouldn't know anything about that."

The controversies over the Supreme Court appointments manifestly were not helpful to the Nixon Administration. Kissinger had not become openly involved in the high-level decisions by Nixon and Attorney General Mitchell on how to handle the Supreme Court, but the Harvard Professor's stature rose indirectly from the Court fight. Nixon told friends after it was all over that Kissinger was such a good adviser that he "knows when not to offer advice."

As Kissinger's stock rose, the President quietly enjoyed all of his aide's personal publicity. At least someone in the Administration might be called colorful. No one else was becoming known for his charisma or glamour. The only showman was Vice President Spiro T. Agnew. The Vice President would launch verbal bombastics at television networks, newspaper publishers, students, Women's Liberation leaders, and anyone else who provoked his ire. If this failed to get a laugh, he would show up on the tennis court or golf course, accompanied by Frank Sinatra or other show-business friends, and climax his performance with a bad shot and an affectionate forgiving remark from a wounded pro.

Nixon had reached out beyond his own conservative branch of the Republican Party by bringing in Kissinger from the Rockefeller camp. On February 11, 1971, he crossed party lines by appointing the suave former Democratic Governor of Texas John B. Connally as Secretary of the Treasury. Connally was one of the heavies in pushing for a new economic policy. The Nixon Administration went to war against inflation with Phase I and Phase II of a wage-price freeze, which produced enormous publicity and not very dramatic results.

The greatest irony of the first term in office for Richard Nixon was his complete reversal as a foe of Communism. Nixon's political success in the Senate and as Vice President was largely based upon his opposition to the Chinese Communists. Therefore it was not surprising that the world flipped when he got on television in July of 1971 and in a spectacular turnabout announced he would go to Peking to promote better relations. Kissinger had won out.

The two-China policy that Kissinger had favored (at least temporarily) and that Nixon was bound to because of his previous statements concerning Formosa, was a flop. Despite U.S. support publicly and in the back rooms of the Security Council, the Chiang Kai-shek government was kicked out of the United Nations.

However inconsistent Nixon's shift in China policy was, as a political move it was clever. Peking probably would have been seated in the United Nations in 1972 anyway, despite American opposition. Chiang Kai-shek as a man and leader had faded, and just about every American realized that a new relationship with China was necessary.

CHAPTER 21

---✠---

CHINA

In the spring of 1971, the world awoke one day to screaming headlines of an international breakthrough. No new governments had been formed, nor had any diplomat made a major treaty. The United States ping-pong team was going inside the China Wall. It was to be a private visit with no United States government participation. Ping-pong is the national sport of China; and the Chinese international team finished first in four out of the seven categories at the last world tournament. The American team was ranked twenty-fourth. Sports buffs believed the statement by the Secretary of the Chinese team, who invited the Americans "so we can learn from each other and elevate our standards of play."

Those concerned with things other than nets and balls and paddles realized that the seemingly innocuous invitation had been thought about for some time. In point of fact, the decision had been made at no lower a level than Mao Tse-tung's private mountain villa, where he decided in March that it was time to lay the groundwork for a meeting with the President of the United States.

The Chinese economy was hurting, and stronger ties were needed with those nations that depended on United States guidance. Also, this was to be the year that Red China got into the United Nations. Every year there had been a vote and each time they had come closer. Ally after ally had deserted the American voting bloc when it came to the question of admission. Only a handful of countries clung to the fiction that Red China was not the real government of China and the one with whom they should deal. Now there was a bright, articulate international power expert at the President's elbow, and he would listen.

The fifteen members of the United States ping-pong team and the three accompanying reporters were never aware that their visit was a prelude to our official bend in the bamboo curtain. It was well publicized that they were the first organized group of United States citizens to really visit China in twenty-five years, but none of them appreciated Chou En-lai's prophecy, "We have opened a new page in the relations of the Chinese and American people."

President Nixon and Henry Kissinger reacted immediately with a series of announcements allowing Americans to deal economically with China on the same basis as with the Soviet Union. The State Department made it evident that the United States would welcome Chinese visitors, and the currency restrictions on American businessmen dealing with China were suddenly abolished.

The ping-pong players arrived, toured, posed, smiled, and left.

On June 30, 1971, President Nixon, in a routine announcement, advised official Washington that his aide, Henry Kissinger, would leave the next day on a ten-day fact-finding mission. The purpose was to visit South Vietnam and other Far Eastern countries to meet with United States officials and foreign representatives on various matters relating to the war and foreign policy. He would return around July 12th and report directly to the President on his conferences in Thailand, India, and Pakistan.

A year and a half before, Nixon had accepted Kissinger's suggestion that a plan be developed to reopen relations with Red China. This was it.

Kissinger spent the first three days of his tour in Saigon routinely reaffirming the Nixon position on the war.

Only one reporter placed any significance on the arrival of John Holdridge, a Far Eastern specialist from the National Security Council who speaks fluent Chinese. The inquisitive Associated Press writer was told that Holdridge was doing background research on the ties between North Vietnam and the Red Chinese.

On July 5th and 6th, Kissinger was in Bangkok posing for pictures with government officials and reassuring foreign friends that the war in Vietnam would soon be over. His next stop was New Delhi, where there were no clear signs of the Indian-Pakistani war that was just a short time away. He attended a large banquet in his honor and made the routine tour of the poverty areas, promising to talk to President Nixon about increasing medical supplies and food for the starving Indians.

The President of Pakistan, General Yahya Khan, knew the secret. On July 8, 1971, Kissinger arrived in Rawalpindi, West Pakistan, seven miles from Islamabad. Suddenly there was a change in Kissinger's itinerary. One of the lower-ranking staff officers calmly advised reporters waiting in Islamabad that Kissinger had some minor stomach trouble and was going to spend a few days recuperating at a remote Pakistani mountain resort. It was the summer headquarters of the Provincial Government and a plush resort area for Pakistani officials and visiting VIP's.

The next morning, provided with top security by the Pakistani government, an unidentified passenger with a handful of aides boarded a Pakistan International Airlines Boeing 707 for Peking. It was Kissinger, accompanied by John Holdridge; Winston Lord, his special assistant; and Richard Smiser, a career foreign service affairs officer who specialized in Southeast Asian problems. Kissinger's personal secretary, Diane Matthews, was left in Pakistan.

When he arrived at Peking Airport, the President's secret emissary was met by a top protocol aide; an interpreter; and Yah Chen-Ying, Vice Chairman of the Military Affairs Commission. Also on hand was Huang Hua, now Peking's delegate to the United Nations and one of the principals in establishing the Kissinger visit. Kissinger was rushed to a meeting with Chou En-lai, and the two talked for nearly eight hours.

China has no difficulty blanking out the press. Foreign reporters are kept at arm's length, and not even the eager French press was around when Kissinger and his party were given a tour of the forbidden city. Then there were more talks. On July 11th, after a final session with Chou En-lai and his aides, Kissinger left for the return flight to Pakistan at 1:00 p.m. From there he went on to Paris for a dinner date and another secret session designed to end the war. Then he went back to Washington.

Many political experts think Richard Nixon guaranteed his reelection on July 15, 1971, in Burbank, California. This town, which has been the butt of "Laugh-in" jokes about Middle America, is the site of NBC's West Coast television studios.

The brief advance notice to the press merely stated that President Nixon would address the nation on a matter of great import. First, the speculation was that there had been a breakthrough in the Paris talks and that Kissinger had arrived home with good news on the negotiations which he had briefly visited in Paris. Then one of the rumors that surround every President took off like a cyclone. It had to do with China, but not even the White House regular reporters who follow the President everywhere knew what was up. Ten minutes before the President went on the air, an Assistant Press Secretary briefed the press corps. Their astonishment and the lack of time prevented any advance story from reaching the air.

The President opened by reminding the country that he was working for a lasting peace and there could be no "stable and enduring peace without the participation of the People's Republic of China and its 750 million people." Nixon calmly announced that he had sent Kissinger to China to meet with Chou En-lai and that the announcement he was about to make would be simultaneously issued by the head of the Chinese government.

"Premier Chou En-lai and Dr. Henry Kissinger, President Nixon's Assistant for National Security Affairs, held talks in Peking from July 9 to 11, 1971. Knowing of President Nixon's expressed desire to visit the People's Republic of China, Premier Chou En-lai, on behalf of the Government of the People's Republic of China, has extended an invitation to President Nixon to visit China at an appropriate date before May 1972.

"President Nixon has accepted the invitation with pleasure.

"The meeting between the leaders of China and the United States is to seek the normalization of relations between the two countries and also to exchange views on questions of concern to the two sides."

As the wire services spread the word of a visit that could mean a major power realignment in the world, the experts took sides. There were those who felt that Russia might overreact in Berlin. The Soviet forces can consistently be counted upon to go on maneuvers in East Berlin whenever any American diplomatic coup occurs. It is their last dramatic show of Communist strength and unity and cannot be ignored by the West Germans and the American government. Others labeled Nixon's move strictly a political gesture to pick up some liberal support in the next election. All seemed to agree that Chiang Kai-shek, the eighty-five-year-old warrior on Formosa, and the remnants of his Chinese nation would be sacrificed; this despite the President's statement that "our action in seeking a new relationship with the People's Republic of China will not be at the expense of our old friends."

Nixon would leave on a journey of peace in the next few months, and the world might sleep a little sounder knowing that threat of war was at least temporarily suspended.

One hour later, Nixon, Kissinger, and a handful of aides celebrated at the plush Perino's Restaurant in Los Angeles. They drank wine and waited for the early edition of the *Los Angeles Times* to see their reviews.

World reaction to President Nixon's announcement that Henry Kissinger had been secretly meeting in China laying the groundwork for Nixon's own visit was immediate. In the puppet state of South Vietnam the government quickly approved, indicating that the President was correct and it was necessary to "normalize relations, even with our foes." Moscow offered no comment. Japan went through the motions of approving, but industrial leaders were sick, thinking that China might challenge the Japanese private domain as the Asian link with American money. The most dramatic reaction came in South Korea, which still exists under the constant threat of Communist troops to its north. The government protested and proclaimed an official day of mourning for Taiwan (also called Formosa). On the tiny island of Formosa, even the most optimistic leaders of the Chiang Kai-shek regime seemed to realize that their struggle was over. Formosa would not survive if the United States dealt with Red China. France and Italy were ecstatic. Even Nixon's Democratic critics in the Congress of the United States spoke out in favor of the announcement. It was probably the most successful political ploy by any contemporary conservative President who needed a chunk of middle liberal support to guarantee his reelection.

The intrigue had begun in April when President Nixon was hosting a stag dinner in the White House. While others were exchanging political jokes and toasting the President's higher ratings in the Gallup popularity poll, Kissinger was in a small office in the West Wing reading a top-secret confidential message handwritten on a scrap of paper. It had been delivered by a neutral but friendly diplomat. The friend had served as an unofficial intermediary between the White House and the Chinese Communists. Kissinger called the private party and talked to Nixon's military aide and said, "Don't let the President go to bed. I must see him; it's imperative." When the dinner guests were gone, the President called Henry and summoned him to the Lincoln sitting room.

After reading the message, Nixon told Kissinger, "They want a very high-level contact, maybe even a summit meeting." For nearly two hours, President and Professor studied the short message over and over, analyzing every word and beginning to formulate a mental draft of a response. They discussed who could go to China and lay the groundwork for the visit. Secretary of State Rogers was too cold. His aides were too inexperienced. Which Ambassador could be effective but discreet?

Forty-eight hours later, while Kissinger was shaving in his office bathroom in the basement of the White House, the President called and said, "You go to China." This was the high point of proof of Nixon's trust in Kissinger. The aide had learned his boss's thinking processes and proven his loyalty so well as to make him the only logical choice for the most delicate diplomatic mission in four decades.

Kissinger was to work out his own logistics, including the mechanics of getting to China undetected, and a cover story as to why he was out of the country. The President was busy with broader policy decisions, and quickly approved the operational plan drafted by Kissinger and his staff. More meetings had to be held so that the personal emissary understood every little thought and nuance that the President wanted to convey to Chou En-lai and maybe even Mao Tse-tung himself.

Ninety days after that first late-night meeting, when the scribbled note arrived at the White House, Kissinger was in Peking. He read the formal statement that he and Nixon had worked on for nearly ten hours. It was short, simple, and clear, and told Chou En-lai that the President of the United States wanted to resurrect a dialogue and relationship that had been dead for twenty years. At the end, Kissinger said Americans were now in the land of mystery, and this meeting could change the future of not only two great powers, but the world.

After reading the statement, Chou En-lai and Kissinger drifted into a discussion of the philosophy of power politics and wondered why nations develop such funny concepts of each other. Chou En-lai liked Kissinger, and Kissinger respected Chou's power. The meetings were held at irregular hours.

The clocks in political chambers during times of delicate diplomatic sessions are as inconspicuous as in Las Vegas hotels. In the gambling houses it is believed that the losers will spot the time and decide they had better go to bed. In times of state negotiations, it is considered rude to inhibit delicate proceedings with reminders of mundane realities such as the hour of the day. At one time Chou En-lai showed up unexpectedly

212

at 4:00 a.m. at Kissinger's hotel suite, with his cadre of inter-preters and bodyguards.

It was a more casual dialogue than had existed between any two major powers in years. Two history-conscious spokesmen could reflect on their own countries' cultures and quietly listen to the problems of the other guy. One of the reasons the talks went so well was Chou En-lai's dignified avoidance of the problems of difference in stature between one who heads a government and one who is merely an aide to a nation's Chief of State.

A sense of humor is a valuable asset. According to the *London Times*, at one point in the negotiations, Chou En-lai rambled on for nearly an hour and then apologized for his wordiness. Kissinger invited him to speak at Harvard, where he said everybody talked an hour without taking a breath.

On October 16, 1971, Henry Kissinger began his second mission to Peking. This time the journey was public. He would arrange the agenda and logistics for President Nixon's trip. The Presidential jet took Kissinger and his staff of nine from Andrews Air Force Base to Hilo, Hawaii, the resort city of America's westernmost state. After that there would be an overnight stop at Guam, and then on to Shanghai and Peking.

The President lent his personal travel staff to Dr. Kissinger for this trip. The Presidential back-up 707 jet was piloted by the President's personal pilot, Colonel Ralph Albertazzie. Air Force Brigadier General James D. Hughes, the top White House military aide, went along, together with Nixon's as-sistant, Dwight L. Chapin. The intricate communications net-work would be handled by Brigadier General Albert Red-mond, chief of the White House Communications Agency. The press would be briefed by Timothy Elbourne, from the White House press secretary's office; and a secret service top aide, Robert H. Taylor, was in charge of security.

Kissinger always trusts his own people more than the State Department's. The only man from State to take the trip was a second-level specialist on mainland China, Alfred Jenkins. He was outranked by three members of Kissinger's National Security Council staff, John H. Holdridge, Winston Lord, and Commander Jonathan Howe.

In between the two Kissinger visits, all hell was breaking loose in China. Internal fights and guesses as to who would take over after Chou En-lai had changed the climate somewhat when Kissinger arrived in October. The Chinese Premier had repeatedly said that Chinese foreign policy would not be affected by internal dissension. That is about as realistic as saying that President Nixon might ignore the polls in an election year.

Chou En-lai had been questioned on his willingness to negotiate with the Soviet Union. Rumors were spreading throughout the world that a breakthrough in American-Chinese relations would be the final straw in splitting Russia and China in the event of world conflict. Chou En-lai, a master politician, put Mao Tse-tung's prestige behind his meetings with the President. Mao was more than a political figure. He had been elevated to a kind of Philosopher Emeritus, and it was difficult for any Chinese politician to question something that the Chairman approved of.

Despite all the threats, there was no real move to pull the rug out from under Chou and his fairly moderate approach to the United States. Kissinger arrived ready to work out details and not expecting any hang-up on the President's forthcoming trip.

One of the problems that is not advertised when the President of the United States goes outside the United States is security. Henry Kissinger knew that, when Richard Nixon was spat upon in South America, a bullet could have gotten to him as easily as saliva. It is traditional to rely upon the host country, Communist or not, to supply ample protection. The theory is they could not afford the embarrassment of an assassination attempt in the eyes of the world. Notwithstanding tradition, it was agreed that the United States would provide its own protection for its Chief Executive, including both secret service and military personnel. The truth as to how many secret guards were used at all times was more closely shielded than the President's departure date. At one point when the President visited a sports event in China, no less than 1,100 security officers were believed to be on duty to make sure that no overzealous young Communist got out of line.

Kissinger was fairly well known when he arrived in China. The blackout in Communist papers about most American achievements was temporarily lifted. He was portrayed as a hero and great thinker. In Communist nations, when the newspapers speak favorably of the visitor, it is a signal to the public that he is welcome, and they may even approach cordiality.

On October 26, 1971, the fight over the Chinese seat to the United Nations ended. The United Nations voted 76 to 35 to seat the Communist government from Peking and to kick out Chiang Kai-shek's Taiwan representative. The United States protested vigorously that both Chinese delegations should be allowed to sit at the international body. But even our allies realized the American spokesmen were just going through the motions, and the expulsion of Taiwan was the natural result of the opening of dialogue between Red China and the United States.

The United States had been a proponent of dual representation. Japan, the Philippines, and other Asian countries that we have defense alliances with agreed. Some of the French-speaking African nations, where Nationalist China has been running technical assistance programs for years, were also loyal. A few of the more dependent middle-of-the-road Latin American countries also stayed in the fold. United Nations Ambassador George Bush had argued for the right of all Chinese people to be represented at the United Nations. He had consulted with Henry Kissinger and other White House aides. Somehow the words never rang quite true. Red China got in and Nationalist China got out.

On November 30th, seven months after the midnight meeting in the White House when President Nixon and Henry Kissinger framed their response to the scribbled note inviting a high-level meeting, Kissinger held a press conference.

Presidential Press Secretary Ronald Ziegler introduced Kissinger and revealed that, "Of course Secretary of State Rogers and Dr. Kissinger will be accompanying the President."

Across town Senator Symington and others who had warned the American people that Kissinger was in reality a Supersecretary of State with fantastic powers and not answering to anybody must have smiled. Kissinger told the press that Chairman Mao would receive the President in Peking and that Nixon would also visit Hangchow and Shanghai. Mrs. Nixon would go along, together with a small working team of top aides.

Kissinger emphasized it would be a working trip, with a series of extended conferences with Chinese leaders. The Presidential aide ducked pressing questions from Peter Lisagor of the *Chicago Daily News* as to whether or not the purpose of the meeting was to end the Vietnam conflict.

The press would push for extensive coverage, but in the beginning it looked as if it might be limited. It turned out to be more extensive than they had hoped for, with most of the world watching by satellite when President and Mrs. Nixon exchanged courtesies with China's leaders. Kissinger told the press that never in China's long history had that ancient land come up with a problem like press coverage of a visit by an American President.

It was interesting to watch Kissinger slip into the trap of offering an opinion as to where the power base was in Communist China. At that press conference, he was specifically asked about internal problems in the Communist government. Kissinger tactfully replied that the visit by the President did not entitle Americans to speculate on the internal conditions in that country. Then the Presidential confessor slipped and revealed that Nixon would be meeting with certain select Chinese aides of Chou En-lai, and he named them. In a country where there is daily competition for who sits to the right and left of the heads of State, Kissinger had inadvertently given stature to a couple of assistants of their politburo bosses.

This is not an unusual diplomatic maneuver. When Kissinger visits Japan or other nations, he meets with the "top candidates" in the forthcoming election. The only gimmick is that those in power get to determine who is a top candidate and who is not. It was as if Mao had arrived in the United States and expressed a desire to meet George McGovern, George Wallace, and Ted Kennedy but left Ed Muskie out. The newspapers and political pundits would have a field day on the omission.

The trip was to be a working visit and not an official diplomatic tour. Kissinger warned the press that there would be little chance of diplomatic relations being established at that time between the United States and the People's Republic of China.

Kissinger had already earned the respect of the Washington press corps by repeatedly demonstrating his ability to sidestep journalists' traps. Sometimes in sidestepping, he trips and

217

says more with his negative than he would with a positive. At that press conference one of the reporters for a New York paper tried to pin down U.S. foreign policy toward China. "You say we recognize the Government of Taiwan. Do we recognize the Government of Taiwan as the government of China?" the reporter asked.

Dr. Kissinger replied, "I have stated the position that both Chinese governments maintain that they represent all of China. We maintain diplomatic relations with the government of Taiwan, and I will not go beyond that."

Kissinger tried to lobby the press into realizing the tremendous significance of the Presidential visit. He reminded the astute newsmen that the two countries had been cut off from each other for twenty-five years, not just in diplomatic contact, but in all other contacts—cultural, journalistic, academic, and so on. It was probably the best opportunity that Henry had had since Nixon's inauguration to point to the President's statesmanship.

But the China trip was a tour de force for Henry A. Kissinger.

Who but Henry Kissinger could have slipped into mainland China, arranged a chat for President Nixon and Chou En-lai and Mao Tse-tung, and kept it all a secret? The *New York Times* applauded Kissinger by declaring that only he could match the Orientals at inscrutability. With all of the missions of Nixon's secret agent now coming to light, none required more fancy footwork, intellect, and intrigue than the negotiations with the Chinese.

On February 20, 1972, Air Force One, which had been renamed The Spirit of '76, taxied out onto the lead runway of Andrews Air Force Base. School children, government employees, well-wishers, television cameramen, security guards, hangers-on, and the curious jammed the public areas of that airport as the President of the United States took off on one of the most historic journeys in contemporary history. The President took a good chunk of Americana with him. Besides Mrs. Nixon, Kissinger, Secretary of State William Rogers, and his pilot Ralph Albertazzie, there was a cross-section of personnel.

The wheels touched down at the Rainbow Bridge Airport in Shanghai at 6:55 a.m., Red Chinese time, on February 21, 1972. The plane was checked, and the man went on to Peking Airport. At 11:30 in the morning, forty-two Chinese officials, headed by Premier Chou En-lai, greeted the President of the United States while the Chinese Army suffered through "The Star-Spangled Banner." A special honor guard of five hundred soldiers, sailors, and airmen was on hand.

The Nixons stayed in a Red Chinese government guesthouse with Presidential Adviser Kissinger and Secretary of State Rogers nearby. Three hours after they arrived, Nixon and Kissinger got down to business and left suddenly for a one-hour meeting with Mao Tse-tung, the philosopher-king of China. Rogers and other members of the official family were relegated to a briefing by a protocol officer. That evening in the Great Hall of the People of China a banquet was held honoring the Nixons.

The next morning the President left to take the thirty-mile trip to see the Great Wall of China and the Ming Dynasty tombs. Then there was a private conference between the President and Chou En-lai, their interpreters and aides, for four hours. The President of the United States is not a ballet buff. He prefers football to concerts, but he politely sat through the Red Detachment of Women that evening at the Oriental version of the Royal Ballet. The next two days brought more meetings at Nixon's guesthouse.

The guts of the China visit were the work sessions between Dr. Henry Kissinger and his Chinese counterpart

Ch'iao Kuan-hua, who carries the title of Deputy Foreign Minister of the People's Republic of China. They were the real diplomats, and they had the task of hammering out a joint communiqué.

It had been nearly twenty-two years since the Communist army had forced Chiang Kai-shck to surrender and established the new China. It had been twenty years since President Truman sent the United States Seventh Fleet to the Taiwan Straits.

Now 750 million Chinese were being asked to once again live in peace with 200 million Americans while hundreds of millions throughout the world depended on that peace. The war in Vietnam would continue, at least for a while; Taiwan would hang on, at least for a little while. Henry Kissinger would remain the second most influential man in the United States of America—and probably not just for a while.

Kissinger, like most men, enjoys the company of beautiful women when traveling. Many international jet setters prefer the guarantees of time-tested companions wherever they go. Others like to sample the unknown.

Henry's second trip to China was well publicized as he set about to shape the agenda for President Nixon's trip. Chinese interpreters would be used, but he insisted on his own team of under-thirty, good-looking secretaries.

In Washington, D.C., an attractive government receptionist, secretary, or clerk is generally expected to be available for a variety of extracurricular activities not outlined in her job specifications. When the President or other top official visits their boss's chambers, they are to be well groomed, well dressed, and well ready for any contingency. When the late Bobby Kennedy was Attorney General, he was prone to make sudden visits to isolated offices in the Justice Department. By the time he left the first surprise stop, the word had reached all potential corridors.

Executives who never remove their coats and formal look hurriedly got rid of their jackets, loosened their ties, rolled up their sleeves, and tried to assume an air of dedicated busyness. More than one good-looking secretary would rush to the ladies' room to unharness and acquire the braless look, which might mean a kind word from the touring Kennedy. At the Pentagon, more than one member of the typing pool has found herself suddenly assigned to a choice job after a shorter-than-usual skirt revealed a good pair of pins to a ranking Defense Department officer. The Pentagon ladies are also the beneficiaries of a constant flow of little gifts from visiting Congressional aides and private contractors who only want a little information or an overdue check to flow more quickly.

Kissinger's post-White House reputation made it necessary for his office to be straight arrow—and it is. There are many sweet young things and some still sweet, but not so young, who fill Washington, D.C.'s, secretarial posts by day and become VIP groupies by night. Our nation's capital ranks highest among major American cities in violent crime and available women.

Hookers starve in Washington, D.C., because of the enthusiastic competition from ranking amateurs who are employed by Uncle Sam but still man-hungry or ambitious.

Kissinger has not gone overboard. In some top administrative offices oversensitive officials only want seasoned ladies of fifty or over, whose skills are good and whose no longer voluptuous bodies guarantee their boss's reputation as a proper family man. A team of under-thirty trim and proper, bright and portable girls carry the title of confidential secretaries to the Presidential Adviser.

Julie Pineau, twenty-four, and Diane Matthews, twenty-nine, go wherever their boss goes. And he goes everywhere. Having survived security clearance checks, the duo seems to hang on despite the game of musical jobs played by other Kissinger staff members.

Their closeness to the boss and awareness of his habits is most noticeable at public functions. Those who don't know Henry will respectfully address him as "Dr. Kissinger," without realizing he strongly prefers to leave the Harvard doctorate in limbo and be called "Mr." Julie and Diane and their *Ladies' Home Journal* wardrobe made the October visit to China with Mr. Kissinger.

After using more aides to transcribe every word of his first twenty hours with Chou En-lai during the secret trip, Kissinger called for his two girls-Friday. Between them they short-handed thirty-five hours of talk so that the President and Kissinger could study every phrase and change of tone in preparing for the Head of State visit. Chinese can be readily translated, but there is no specified English description for the proper but almost humbly fatalistic manner that many Chinese assume in espousing their philosophy. Kissinger's virtuoso secretaries were able to help in reconstructing an essentially accurate picture. Someone had suggested filming the talks so that Nixon and psychological advisers could watch the mannerisms of their host, but the idea was junked as too commercial and flamboyant for Chou's simple tastes.

According to one informed newsman, Kissinger was worried about his reputation as a constant companion to sexy movie star types. He felt the need to present himself as far more conservative in his dealings with the Chinese. Middle America wouldn't tolerate Jill St. John's cleavage in the departure picture of a Presidential emissary on a highly sensitive mission. At times like that, Kissinger worries about his 1964 divorce and how officials in a nation where divorce is highly unusual will react to him. Much of the glib, smooth manner is a cover-up for the insecurity that anyone facing a monumental assignment fears.

Kissinger describes his team of young ladies as magnificent representatives of young American womanhood. Julie and Diane are accustomed to his flattery and dismiss the compliments, pointing out that he literally says that "to all the girls." Julie has the well-scrubbed look of a debutante who has cost daddy a bundle in finishing school, college, European trips, and sports cars. Her father is a well-known Washingtonian, an executive at the Smithsonian Institution. As Henry's private secretary, Julie handles chores that any busy bachelor hands down to a trusted helper. She balances his checkbook (high four figures), orders his groceries (although he almost always eats out), and sends out his cleaning. She keeps his inner-sanctum bathroom stuffed with cologne and shaving cream. Kissinger was recently approached by a major razor manufacturer who wanted to substitute the White House brand of manliness for baseball players in their ads. They didn't get beyond Julie.

Diane Matthews is very much a Virginia lady, with a high civil service rank for her age, and carries the title of Business Secretary to Henry Kissinger. Both girls have suddenly found themselves on the invitation list of Embassy, industry, and private social events whose hosts believe the political adage that the way to a man is through his secretary.

Both of Kissinger's ladies-in-waiting are ending two years of service in the National Security office. Julie accompanied her boss during the surreptitious July, 1971, visit when Kissinger slipped out of Pakistan and into Red China. Diane was left behind to lend authenticity to the cover story of the stomach ache.

The itinerary during the October visit included a taste of tourism. Chinese protocol officials wisely felt that the two

White House secretaries could break the ice for Pat Nixon when she accompanied the President on his official visit.

Julie lost her cool when invited to visit a traditional Chinese clinic. After being gowned and masked, they were led into the operating room where a man was having a lung operation with acupuncture "anesthesia." The 2,000-year-old Chinese medical process known as acupuncture is rapidly getting recognition in the United States and throughout the world. But the insertion of stainless steel needles into the body at key points, followed by forced rotation by the acupuncturist, was too much for the tastes of a squeamish young deb from Maryland. Julie fainted.

Kissinger will never win an award for employee relations. He goes through assistants quicker than some of his girl friends change gowns. At least one former top aide went from Henry's White House office to a rest home. Another was transferred to a foreign service post in oblivion after he couldn't take the Kissinger work pace.

He kept his reputation as a tough taskmaster during the China trip. Diane and Julie were required to transcribe all official meetings and to prepare interim memos for the President in between sessions. Diane uses the traditional Gregg shorthand system. Much to the chagrin of the business college traditionalists, Julie manages as a highly paid personal secretary with just speedwriting.

When the girls returned from China they were invited to publish their impressions in the *Ladies' Home Journal*. This required authorization from both Kissinger and the President himself. The White House generally frowns on first-person articles by staff members, and this request was carefully reviewed by key Presidential advisers. Although the first reaction was a unanimous one, a member of the Press Secretary's office convinced other aides to favor publication of the interview for political reasons. He pointed out that the two clean-cut secretaries saying nice things about their boss might help offset both the swinger reputation and the rumors of Kissinger's merciless treatment of employees. Secondly, the *Ladies' Home Journal* was the right kind of publication to try to gain American female interest in the President's China trip during a crucial election year.

After hours of conferences, the word came down permitting the two Kissinger secretaries to have their memories of China appear with a Ralph Nader exposé and a Sophia Loren cooking lesson in "The magazine women believe in."

Finally, the secret document was published and literate Americans were able to slip behind the bamboo curtain with the White House campfire girls. They revealed such diplomatic delicacies as the fact that the Chinese served the girls yogurt with breakfast. They also ate sesame seed cookies and sweet millet with lotus seed. The magazine editor and the White House are both silent on how much money the girls were paid for their juicy tidbits. The magazine does admit preparing clothes for both secretaries for a picture layout and letting them keep the wardrobe.

Amidst their memories of the China Wall and Chinese orchards was a sprinkling of compliments for their boss and the White House line on how some of our best friends are Chinese Communists.

President Nixon had utilized all of his polished Madison Avenue public relations techniques to shift emphasis on the China trip from political hypocrisy to progress toward world peace. The drama of having Kissinger's report to the press off the record added to the story of intrigue. It would be the President himself who would reveal on network television the full story when the time was right. It was hoped that the result would be that the public would forget that Nixon had led the verbal attacks upon the Chinese Communist nation and demanded that we stay with our ally on Formosa. The American public is a sucker for human interest episodes, and the story of the Pakistan side trip, the stomach ache, and the sneak visit into China would keep even the most prestigious newspapers interested. Then they might not editorialize about the diplomatic turnaround that Nixon was engineering.

Immediately after the President's return from the China conferences, critics began looking around to determine whether or not the visit, at a cost of several hundred thousand dollars and some political standing with select allies, was really worthwhile. The best evidence of the trip's value was in the repeated attacks upon the United States by the Chinese Communist leaders within days after Mr. Nixon's departure.

One month after the leaders of two nations had smiled, shaken hands, and hinted that diplomatic relations might be restored in the near future, the Chinese Premier was sharply attacking the United States position in Vietnam. Chou accused Nixon of sabotaging the Paris peace talks, and continued to spew out the Communist line that had kept the two nations apart for two and one-half decades.

The economic superstructure in the United States is a strange and complex animal. It moves slowly and then jets ahead suddenly in response to a political opening created by a White House announcement. In this case, those who make millions through import-export regulations on various products began to make their move within forty-eight hours after Nixon's return from China.

Pitches were made to Red Chinese economic advisers by American business trying to capitalize on the hesitancy to use Japanese products. Oddly enough, despite the American losses suffered thirty years ago in World War II, this country has not hesitated to gobble up everything made in Japan that costs a little less than our own products. Not so in China, where the memories of generations of war and distrust would affect economic policy whether the Communists were in control or not.

226

Henry Kissinger had cautioned reporters that diplomatic relations would not be established at this meeting. He had said repeatedly that it was a preliminary series of talks, and no one should expect a major turnabout in relations overnight. Yet, even Kissinger in his protestations about moving slowly may not have anticipated that the Chinese Communists would turn around and clobber the President of the United States and our entire military operation in Vietnam, as well as our diplomats in Paris, almost before the Spirit of '76 engines had died down from Nixon's return trip to Washington.

It is pretty well agreed among political scientists in this country that Richard Nixon's political background and intellect would not combine to give birth to a plan including a unilateral effort to restore relations with the Chinese Communists. Unquestionably, the Strangelovian dreams of Dr. Kissinger for internationalism were responsible for the whole project. It was Kissinger who first brought the scribbled memo from his intermediary urging the secret trip. It was Kissinger who, after extensive visits with the President discussing who might go as an advance man, ended up taking the trip himself. It was Kissinger who hammered out the preliminary notice and set up the itinerary and basis for the talks between Nixon and Chou En-lai, as well as Mao Tse-tung. It was Kissinger again who was called upon, not only to read the joint communiqué after the conferences, but to explain it.

It is safe to say that history will record that this one-shot effort to liberalize U.S. policy toward the most populous Communist nation in the world was the brain child of the President's Adviser-on-Everything. Coupled with its arrival at the United Nations, and the sulking exit by Formosa's delegates, the visit by the President of the United States had given the People's Republic of China a new-found stature in the eyes of the world.

In New York, pictures of Chiang Kai-shek which adorned

227

those restaurants and bars that members of the Formosa delegations frequented were quickly taken down. They would not
be ostentatiously replaced with pictures of Mao, but some current sceneries of mainland China appeared within days. The
small independent American businessman does not have time
for international politics.

While Kissinger and President Nixon were touring the
great China Wall, a member of the Chinese Communist secret
police was visiting in Washington, D.C., with State Department security officials discussing the arrival of Communist
diplomats in New York. There is a fiction that New York
City police are the only ones concerned with the well-being of
the diplomats attending United Nations sessions. In reality, the
principal decisions concerning Heads of State and controversial Ambassadors are made jointly by the State Department
and Pentagon officers. Fortunately, none of the members of
the new China delegation were well known as individuals, and
it was doubtful that the supporters of the Formosa government
or the routine protesters would try anything out of the ordinary. Only when a Castro or a Khrushchev comes to New
York do government agencies seriously consider that there is
danger of an assassination attempt.

The busiest office at the United Nations for two weeks
would be the printing department. It was their job to make
sure, as if by magic, the names of the Formosa delegation
would suddenly disappear and the Red Chinese spokesmen
would just as suddenly become entrenched in the full gamut of
international activity at United Nations headquarters.

Is it not ironic that a delegation of one of the great powers
of the world arrived in New York clothed with diplomatic immunity and passes to the United Nations; yet, technically
speaking, the United States did not recognize their country's
existence and could not even go through the routine of diplomatic relations?

CHAPTER 22

———————— ✠ ————————

SECRET AGENT

President Nixon enjoys watching a football game and calling up the coach with suggestions for new plays. He never made it as a ball player at Whittier College, but recently he has become the quarterback of the roughest worldwide game of all. His running back is Henry Kissinger. In fact, Nixon's code name throughout the dozen secret meetings between Kissinger and the North Vietnamese was "Quarterback."

Asking Henry Kissinger, whose face has appeared on the cover of as many magazines as the President's, to be a secret agent seems about as plausible as expecting that Jane Fonda could stroll down Fifth Avenue topless and unrecognized. The ostentatious Presidential aide is constantly in the company of beautiful women, continuously surrounded by Secret Service bodyguards, and often followed by the nation's most inquisitive reporters. Yet Nixon selected Kissinger for the most important role in the Presidential aide's lifetime—concerted efforts to end the Vietnam war by secret meetings. It was agreed that Nixon would keep in close contact with Kissinger, both by radio and with memorandums shuttled back and forth by Kissinger's close-mouthed deputy, Brigadier General Alexander Haig.

Henry was not too elusive when escorting Hollywood's

finest to a variety of nightspots; but he outdid himself by shuttling back and forth to Paris from Washington, D.C., between August 4, 1969, and September 13, 1971, with as much ease as some men drive to and from the office.

When President Nixon, in a television spectacular, revealed Kissinger's secret meetings, it caught even Washington's sophisticated newsmen totally by surprise. The revelation made the celebrated Chinese caper seem routine. Evidently, the art of secret diplomacy is alive and well, and Kissinger is its foremost protagonist.

In a desperate pursuit of peace in Vietnam and the domestic tranquility Nixon required for reelection, Kissinger made twelve furtive trips to Paris in thirty months. The clandestine diplomacy flopped, and so Nixon hoped by making it public he could embarrass the North Vietnamese into some kind of meaningful negotiation and save a little face with the millions of Americans who were sick and tired of the war.

It had been decided right after Nixon took office that the public spotlight would prevent effective negotiations to end the war. A frank exchange without the pressures of publicity was needed, and so Kissinger was dispatched in the role of secret agent.

After the President's revelation, Kissinger came forward to share his modus operandi in super-secret diplomacy. "I don't want to go into all of the details of how it was done," Kissinger told a press conference, "because we may want to do it again." Despite the seriousness of purpose and the lack of success, the Presidential adviser basked in the glory of his new role as an intellectual James Bond. Agent OOHenry first met with his North Vietnamese counterpart on August 4, 1969. Five more comparable meetings were held during the next year and a half, with little success and not even a hint of acceptance of any of the American proposals. On May 31, 1971, President

Nixon holidayed for the Memorial Day weekend at Camp David. Kissinger was in Paris delivering a message from the President which offered to set a "deadline for the withdrawal of all American forces in exchange for the release of all prisoners of war and a ceasefire." Top Republican advisers to the President were optimistic and felt that they could pull the rug out from under the Democrats, and reelection was a cinch. The war would be over as Nixon promised, and the United States would not have sacrificed too much glory. But the North Vietnamese said no.

On June 26, 1971, Kissinger flew quietly to meet Sir Burke Trend, Secretary of the British Cabinet. Supposedly, they were to discuss cooperation with the National Security Council. Actually, it was a cover-up for another meeting with the stubborn North Vietnamese delegation.

Three weeks later, Kissinger got his famous belly ache in Pakistan and flew to Peking to lay the groundwork for the summit meeting between President Nixon and Chou En-lai. He also found time for his famous dinner date with Margaret Osmer at a Paris restaurant. Associated Press correspondents thought they really had a scoop in discovering the intimate rendezvous between the Presidential aide and the CBS producer. Actually, Kissinger was delighted with the discovery, since it helped obscure his real purpose in France.

The tenth meeting (on July 26, 1971) was easy. With Nixon in Camp David and the Apollo space mission in progress, nobody missed Henry. Three weeks later on August 16th, the country was trying to figure out the new economic program that the President had announced the night before. Nobody noticed Kissinger departing from Andrews Air Force Base.

It was agreed by the President and top aides that major domestic announcements would be timed so as to provide ample cover for Henry's missions. Accordingly, on September 13, 1971, Phase II of the new economic program was announced and, while the President met with the nation's business and labor leaders, Kissinger sneaked off to Paris.

The original logistics had been arranged by a close friend of Henry's, Jean Saintany, former French Commissioner in Hanoi. The French foreign minister, Maurice Schumann, contacted his nation's leading television and newspaper executives in order to play down coverage of American involvement in the Vietnam talks.

For a typical secret mission, Super Agent would leave his Washington apartment on a Sunday morning after a well-publicized social Saturday night. The press and the curious would assume that Henry, like every other swinger, was sleeping late. Actually, he would be picked up at dawn by Secret Service men and driven to Andrews Air Force Base. There an unmarked C135 aircraft with elaborate communications gear kept under top security was made available. The regular flow of military and diplomatic air traffic made the takeoff seem routine. Presidential aides do not go through customs. Can you imagine some overeager French official asking Henry Kissinger, "How long do you intend to be in France, and what is the purpose of your visit?"

The first stop would usually be West Germany and most likely the Rhein-main Air Base near Frankfurt. After that six-hour flight, Kissinger would change to a Lockheed Jetstar for a 72-minute flight to a small French military airport. The small remote airstrip nine miles southwest of Paris borders a village which does little more than eat cheese for excitement.

For several weeks, the townsfolk noticed strangers in increasing numbers, as the French secret police provided extra protection for President Nixon's secret emissary. Despite the remoteness of the airstrip and lack of air traffic, the plane would taxi to the far end and unload its distinguished passenger to a waiting black Citroen DS 21 with curtains and bulletproof glass. A small caravan of security guards and Kissinger aides would then travel with the man to the lower-middle-class town of Choisy-le-Roi. There Kissinger would rest in a private home and change cars for the short drive to the villa, where he would meet with the North Vietnamese.

Each time Nixon called on Kissinger for a new mission, it became apparent to those who shared the secret that never before in contemporary American history had a President so substantially relied on the talents and energies of another. He had been known as "Henry the K," "Henry the Kiss," "The Professor," "Herr Doctor," and "Super-Kraut." But the label never changed the product, and this German-born Harvard prodigy literally juggled the future peace of the world in between personal pursuits.

John Foster Dulles had run a one-man Department of State for Eisenhower; but, after all, he was the Secretary of State. Kissinger's authority and awesome influence on the President are centered on the National Security Council, which codifies military and political plans and creates the options for America's future. He had been the President's stabilizer from the beginning. Now he was the all-purpose emissary expected to express what the President was thinking as clearly and effectively as if Nixon were present, and maybe then some.

The President limited details of Kissinger's missions to a handful of top government officials. The only members of the select circle who knew what Henry was doing were Kissinger's top aide, Brigadier General Haig; his most trusted adviser, Winston Lord (the fastest pen in the Kissinger stable); Nixon's Press Secretary Ronald Ziegler, who came up with cover stories if newsmen inquired about Kissinger's where-

233

abouts; Secretary of State William Rogers, who had become politically impotent; and Presidential Aide Robert Haldeman.

When the President of the United States mentions the Chief Executive of any other nation, half a dozen countries squirm. One adjective or a little bit of emphasis can shift the stock market, foreign trade, and has been known to upset and overturn a small government. It was curious, to say the least, when the President opened his nationwide talk about the secret visits by thanking President Georges Pompidou for his assistance. But it was President Pompidou who had authorized Jean Saintany to work with Kissinger. Saintany had been friendly with the late Ho Chi Minh of North Vietnam.

When Kissinger finally arrived for each visit at the private villa where the talks would take place, he was accompanied by a trio of Americans—his aide, Winston Lord; a translator; and a mystery man whom to this day no one has named. Kissinger would sit in a sparsely furnished living room and face the five-man delegation from North Vietnam, headed by Le Duc Tho and his deputy Xuan Thuy.

On one occasion the special French secret police contingent thought the house was being guarded by a group of local gendarmes who had been assigned, but the local police had been called to a student demonstration some miles away. The house was unguarded when a group of touring American students knocked on the door to request shelter from a sudden French rainstorm. Inside, a dozen top officials of two nations wondered who should answer the door. Finally, the fast-thinking translator for the Kissinger team opened the door and told the students the house was quarantined with measles. They peddled their bikes away, having come within a few feet of discovering the most important diplomatic secret of the century. The sergeant in charge of the local gendarmes was relieved of duty.

The meetings with the North Vietnamese were always polite and never hostile, but little was agreed upon other than recognizing their differences. Often Kissinger would take a break and walk alone with one or two of the North Vietnamese in the secluded gardens of the villa. There they talked about soccer, the history of Germany, and Kissinger's reputation with the ladies of the world. When it was the Vietnamese turn to host, they served ChaGio, which is a snack of fish covered with rice and dipped in a smelly fish oil. Sometimes the Vietnamese delegation would excuse themselves and debate one another over interpretation of a Kissinger point, and when they returned they were unified.

They behaved correctly. "Their personal behavior was impeccable, and I have great respect for them as individuals. They were tough, tenacious, yet courteous," Kissinger reported. After each meeting Kissinger would retrace his steps with the kind of deliberation you use when you have lost your wallet and do not remember where. He would drive in one car back to the Villa Coublay airport and fly to Frankfurt. There he would transfer to the big jet and begin dictating his report during the transatlantic flight to Washington. He would use the radio to summarize for General Haig, who in turn took the messages to "Quarterback."

Crossing the time zone several times, Kissinger would arrive home for dinner Monday night and be taken directly to the White House. His meeting with the President ranged from one to seven hours, and his briefings were analogous to the teacher who kept students after class to make sure they understood each point.

As luck would have it, not only was there no leak from the White House or from the North Vietnamese, but the French surprisingly kept quiet. Only a mechanical problem on one of the flights threatened the ultrasecret nature of the Kissinger

235

trip. A forced landing was made at a United States air base en route, and the hydraulic system quickly repaired. No one deplaned.

During ten of the twelve secret meetings, it was kept secret that Kissinger was in Paris. Twice, however, he went out of his way to be seen. Anyway, the press knew Henry was in Paris and thought nothing of it. After all, the world's most famous swinger was entitled to be in the City of Love.

During a few of the visits there were moments of hope, but the trips ended up disastrously unsuccessful. A University of Michigan economist tried to figure up the cost to the American taxpayer of the abortive twelve meetings and, after considering flying time, the salaries of those involved, expenses (not including dinner for Margaret Osmer), communications equipment, radio and transatlantic calls, etc., it came to somewhat in excess of two million dollars.

The war in Vietnam has produced many firsts, not the least of which is a world's record in Vietnam peace plans produced—none of which seem to work. When President Nixon announced that his globe-trotting top aide had been trying for two years through secret diplomacy to end the war, he picked up a few points with middle-of-the-roaders who thought Nixon had too hard a line; but the drama of Kissinger's secret flights did not change the fact that the war was still going on. The thirteenth meeting was set for November 20, 1971. It was called off suddenly when Le Duc Tho, North Vietnam's top negotiator, called in sick. Unlike airline stewardesses, there are no others on standby.

Nixon told the nation on January 25, 1972: "Two months have passed since they called off that meeting, and the only reply to our plan has been an increase in troop infiltration . . . our proposal for peace was answered by a step-up of the war

236

on their part." That was the reason Nixon said that he was making the meetings and peace proposals public.

The thrust of the various proposals that Kissinger carried to Paris was based on total withdrawal from South Vietnam in six or nine months. Also an exchange of prisoners was to begin the day an agreement was reached. Of equal import were the ceasefire and new elections for South Vietnam. Nixon had persuaded President Nguyen Van Thieu to resign a month before new elections and to allow the Vietcong to take part. Still there was no agreement.

Nixon was angry and confused and embarrassed. He had gone further than he ever thought he would in compromising to end the war. Yet, the enemy was berating America at public sessions and not responding in private.

It took many months to convince President Thieu to agree that the Vietcong and National Liberation Front could participate in elections "as long as they gave up violent actions." Communism is against the law in South Vietnam. They have the Constitutional admonition that many Americans act as if we had.

In the few years since Nixon and Kissinger had taken the reins of American foreign policy, no fewer than eight plans had been offered to end that war—and none of them had been responded to with anything more than abuse.

Most of the negotiations end up with the basic all-or-nothing argument. The United States wanted the political future of South Vietnam agreed upon before withdrawal; North Vietnam insisted on withdrawal first and talk later.

Nixon announced that, "The only thing our plans do not do is to have the United States join our enemy to overthrow our ally, which the United States will never do."

Kissinger is often photographed, but seldom heard. Some

237

of the President's advisers still fear American public reaction to the heavy German guttural accent that seems to be the humanization of Dr. Strangelove. But once in a while it becomes necessary to take Kissinger's voice out of the closet and allow him to do more than nod and smile.

Two days after President Nixon's startling revelations about the dozen secret meetings, Kissinger was allowed to speak out. A news conference was held in which Kissinger outlined the proposals for peace in Indochina and talked about his trips. He started by reminding everyone that finding a solution to the war is the issue of greatest concern to the Administration, but that there must be a just settlement.

Three months before the Republican Convention of 1972, the Vietnam War accelerated. Massive attacks by the Vietcong were evoking beefed-up American retaliation attacks. The on-again off-again air strikes were resumed. And the American people, tired of the war's frustration, were made fully aware that the Secret Agent's journeys had been totally in vain up to that point. But by summer, Kissinger was again shuttling back and forth across the Atlantic in yet another effort to find a satisfactory settlement of the war.

EPILOGUE

One of the problems in writing a contemporary biography is that the printer cannot keep up with the subject. Just as one adventure of Super-Kraut is recorded, another pops up.

As this book is being completed, the world is asked to accept a new promise of peace. A Kissinger masterminded summit in Moscow has been held. A new treaty between the United States and Russia has been signed. The chances of nuclear holocaust may have been reduced a little.

At the Dniepto Hotel in Teheran, Iran, Henry Kissinger talked with William Dingle of the Gannett News Service on May 30, 1972. They were on the stopover in Iran on the way home with President Nixon from the historic Moscow meeting.

Kissinger had been at the President's elbow during the meeting with the Soviet leaders. He shot down any wild dreams of miracles in an unrehearsed briefing. "One of the things we said to each other early was, 'Don't let's surprise each other at the Summit.' . . . So I suppose the price you pay is that it tends to run along the course that you have charted. . . . We don't look for the unexpected."

After the interview Henry Kissinger joined the President in a toast to Iran's Shah. The traditional belly dancer appeared

239

and entertained. At the end of her act, she did the unexpected, and plopped into Kissinger's lap.

Unperturbed by the incident, Henry said, "We went to Russia to keep the world safe for girls like this. . . ."

DATE D